Two Plays

DAMNED FOR DESPAIR
DON GIL OF THE GREEN BREECHES

John Croft

First published in 1992 by Absolute Classics, an imprint of
Absolute Press, 14 Widcombe Crescent, Bath, England
01225 316013
© Laurence Boswell

Cover and text design: Ian Middleton

Photoset and printed by
The Longdunn Press Ltd, Bristol

ISBN 0 948230 55 X

DAMNED FOR DESPAIR

Adapted and Translated by Laurence Boswell
with Jonathan Thacker

DON GIL OF THE GREEN BREECHES

Adapted and Translated by Laurence Boswell
with Deirdre McKenna

Two plays by
Tirso de Molina

a b s o l u t e c l a s s i c s

INTRODUCTION

Tirso de Molina (1580–1648) was indisputably one of the great dramatists of the Spanish seventeenth century – the Golden Century. Some rank him as the greatest – and, given his ability to create mythic figures like don Juan (his *El burlador de Sevilla* is the prototype don-Juan play), intensely human works like the biblical tragedy *La venganza de Tamar* or the tragicomedy *El condenado por desconfiado (Damned for Despair)*, or outrageous comedies like *Don Gil de las calzas verdes (Don Gil of the Green Britches)*, it is easy to see why.

On the face of it, Tirso's life was rather different from that of other Spanish writers of his day in that he became a friar (of the Order of Mercy) probably before he was twenty-one whereas Lope de Vega and Calderón sowed some scandalous wild oats before taking minor orders in their old age. However, such a view shows the danger not only of trying to see the author behind the pen but also of assuming that a seventeenth-century monk must have had a monkish outlook on life. Not for nothing was Tirso censured and banished from Madrid in 1625 by a Government watchdog (La Junta de Reformación de Costumbres) for writing 'secular plays' that were 'notorious incitements to vice'. Though this was obviously unjust insofar as some were unimpeachable saint-plays or high-profile dramatisations of basic Christian truths, such as *Damned for Despair*, many – he published over 200 plays and may have written some 400 – offer gleeful spectacles of the conventionally pious and upright slipping on banana skins craftily set down for them by young lovers out to get their way by hook or crook, as Dona Juana does in *Don Gil of the Green Britches*.

For some three centuries, this kind of watchdog slant (that the real Tirso was to be found in his more conformist religious plays such as *La prudencia en la mujer*) held sway. The comedies were seen as little more than witty doodlings and then, latterly, as equally conformist sermons in comic disguise. Perhaps at least what actual stagings of his plays, (not least The Gate's Spanish Golden Age 1991/2 season,) have shown is that the real playwright – for all his illustrious achievements as friar Gabriel Téllez – had a professional genius for providing professional actors with dramas teeming with opportunities to enact 'liberal', Christian fundamentalist attitudes in a persuasive light. The Gate's realizations showed that *Damned for Despair* and *Don Gil* are both in their different ways excellent examples of Tirso's performance potential.

The Spanish title, *El condenado por desconfiado* conveys not only a warning about giving in to despair and self-doubt but also the converse, 'El salvado por confiado': the basic Christian belief that, through unmerited grace, anyone can be saved provided he has faith ('confiado') and good works to his credit. The play raises issues of wilful evil, Faustian deals with the Devil, freedom and predestination, the need to condemn the sin and respect the sinner even, astonishingly, when he was a foul bandit like Enrico with the bare minimum of good works (loving respect for his father). But the fundamental idea behind this bandit-turned-saint topic, a favourite one in Spanish culture, is the Augustinian argument that the exceptionally wicked have within them the guts to become far better persons than the average person can hope to be.

The Spanish title *Don Gil de las calzas verdes* also implies more than the English version does: 'Gil' had long been a literary name for a rustic, 'don' a sought-after title denoting nobility, so that anyone with his head screwed on would realize at once that 'don Gil' is a fanciful and absurd contradiction. Add to that the symbolic meaning of green as sexual craving, and the play's central scene in Act Three where four well-bred, noble characters all appear in green breeches aping the 'real' don Gil who, as every Tom, Dick and Harry in the audience knows, is not don Gil at all, becomes classic farce exposing the exalted as no better than you or me.

JACK SAGE

DAMNED FOR DESPAIR

8

DAMNED FOR DESPAIR received its British première at the Gate
Theatre, Notting Hill on 16th November 1991. The cast was as
follows:

PAULO	Timothy Walker
PEDRISCO	Mark Sproston
THE DEVIL	Simon Gregor
LIZARDO	Bob Barrett
OCTAVIO	Richard Sandells
CELIA	Saira Todd
LIDORA	Tilly Tremayne
ENRICO	Lorcan Cranitch
GALVAN	Mark Spalding
ESCALANTE	Shaun French
CHERINOS	Robin Sneller
ANARETO/ALBANO	Tim Barlow
THE GOVERNOR/THE JUDGE	Christopher Pollard
SHEPHERD	Harry Peacock
ANGEL	Edward Rose
PEASANTS, MILITIA, BANDITS & PRISONERS	Peter Graham
	David Ellis
	Eden Jane Eyre
	Carmel Morrissey
	Rob Orange
	Martin Cook
	Mark Kelly
	Bev Popely

Constance Byam-Shaw
Francisco Figueredo

DIRECTOR	Stephen Daldry
DESIGNER	Tim Hatley
LIGHTING DESIGNER	Ace McCarron
MUSIC	Stephen Warbeck
PRODUCER	Caroline Maude

DAMNED FOR DESPAIR was commissioned with the support of the Arts Council of Great Britain and the LWT Plays on Stage Award.

FOR LOTTIE

Cue 0 blackout

ACT ONE

SCENE ONE

LXQ1 — after tableau formation
Lx R2 — As Paulo crosses

A mountain, forests, and two caves.

Enter Paulo.

PAULO: This home of mine is blessed!
I live in happy solitude,
On the side of this mountain,
Protected from wind and rain,
By this thick dark forest,
Where my only guests are
Trees, birds, and grass.
Now the dawn is breaking,
Dabbing the grass with light,
Each blade seems to bow
In respect before the sun,
Who rides his golden chariot
Through the shadow of night,
Cutting through the darkness,
With his swords of pure light.
And now as I stare up
To that pale blue carpet,
Trodden by His holy feet,
I wish that I could see,
Wish I could tear a
Tiny hole in those folds
Of bright blue tissue,
Just to see, just to see. . . .
But this will drive me mad.
Dear Lord, I know I can't
Look upon Your holy face,
As you look down upon us,
From Your throne of light,
Where you're served by angels,
Whose beauty is more radiant,
Than the light of the sun.
My Lord, I want to praise You
For all Your gifts of love,
But how can my humble prayer

LxQ 3

Compare with all Your beauty?
How can I thank You for
Revealing my vocation?
How can I thank You for
Taking me from the world,
The sinful world of man,
Which is a stairway leading
Down to the Gates of Hell.
O my divine Master,
How can I thank You for
Showing me to the path
Which if I can follow,
Will lead me to Your heart?
And how can I thank You
For giving me this blessed home?
Here delicate birds sing
Hymns of love to You and
Bullrushes and thyme bushes
Blown by the wind echo
Their lullabies and I cry:
The beauty of this world
Is indescribable,
What then of Heaven's beauty?
Here the gentle streams
Like shards of diamond
Glitter in the meadow
Darting light into my soul,
Reflecting Your pure love
Into the darkness of my heart.
And here wild mountain flowers
Perfume the fugitive wind
With fragrant scents and
Fertilise the meadows
With the seeds of new life.
I'm silenced by Creation,
A work more beautiful
Than anything man can make,
A miracle which must
Stop the mouths of poets.
So, divine Master, for the
Joy You pour into my soul,
And for all the holy gifts
With which my days are blessed,

I give You humble thanks,
And promise to serve You,
Constantly in a life of prayer.
I promise to serve You
Taking no pleasure in
The sinful world below,
However wide its doors,
Are opened in temptation.
And please, dear Master,
I beg You on my knees,
Help me to persevere,
Help me resist all sin,
Without You I won't succeed:
Man is made of vile clay,
Man is made of brittle clay.

He goes back into his cave.

SCENE TWO

Enter Pedrisco. L×Q4

He carries a very large bundle of grass, twigs and other vegetation.

PEDRISCO: Enter me, with donkey food,
Grasses, twigs and shrubbery,
If I eat all this greenery,
I see an awful end for me,
And it won't be constipation.
God did You create me
To eat the food You made,
For donkeys, cows and grubs?
If You did, then send me
The patience: not to
Mention the digestion,
To endure such a fate.
It's all my mother's fault!
When I fell into the world
From between her fat thighs,
She said, "Oh my baby,
You've the eyes of a saint."
So that's what I'm supposed

To be, thank God I never
Married, think what a
Mother-in-law might suggest.
Good Lord, I understand
Sainthood is an honour but
Hunger's a strange blessing.
Forgive me this frailty, Lord,
Forgive my weak belly.
Now, as I've confessed my sins,
Could I call on Your mercy
And make a small suggestion.
If you remove my yearnings,
I'll be a better hermit,
Sainthood would be easy.
Oh Lord, another request:
Could I beg a dispensation
To forget about fasting.
I like to eat big dinners,
And fat people need a saint.
Ten years ago I left home,
And came here with Paulo,
He lives in that cave and
This is my hermitage.
Here we do our penance,
Eating grass, twigs, and shrubs.
I'm sad when I think of the
Plenty I've left behind,
And the nothing I have here.
Sometimes as the waterfall
Splashes out a sad tune,
I sing a lament to
Some old friends in Naples:
"Oh pigs of my back yard
Take pity on your master,
You pigs of my back yard,
Oh where are you now?"
When I walked down stone streets
And not over rocks and roots,
You were so sensitive
To every rumble of
My big hungry belly.
Oh you were so loyal,
Giving bacon, chops and ham

Now I never see a snout.
Well, hunger's beaten me again,
I'll have to go and eat,
As I say grace over
This grassy feast, I'll beg
Heaven for protection,
Because after such a meal,
My belly swells so much
That I think I'm pregnant and
Sometimes I'm terrified
That I might give birth
To a whole flock of sheep.
And sometimes I imagine I
Might give birth to the Spring,
I've eaten so many seeds.
Ooh Paulo's coming out of his cave,
I'd better dive into mine,
And fill up with fodder.

SCENE THREE

Enter Paulo in great distress.

PAULO: I'm defeated by a dream!
Death came to my cave,
And drove me from prayer,
The dream told a story
Which burns in my soul.
Have I offended God or
Is this the Devil's dream?
As I knelt in meditation
Death danced about me
Swinging her scythe through me
Without breaking my flesh.
Oh God in Heaven help me.
Then she lay down her scythe
And loaded the arrow
Which ends all human courage,
Her right hand gripped the bow
Then she shot through my heart.
I watched my chest split,

Watched drops of blood sink
And saw my body falling
Like a beast in the slaughter.
Then my soul flew away
And I saw the face of God,
The face I've lived to see,
Oh, it was hard and cold,
Brutal and unmoving.
In His hand He held a sword,
At His side the Devil,
Smiling at a victory,
For he had won my soul.
Satan read out my sins,
Whilst Michael, who guards the
Newly dead, spoke of my
Good deeds; in the scales
My life was weighed, the left
Scale came down fast while
The right leapt up and so
God pointed down to Hell,
And my soul began to fall
To the place of terror.
I woke up from my dream,
Shaking on the cave floor,
In a pool of freezing sweat,
With the smell of rotting
Flesh burning in my nose.
What does this dream mean?
Does it predict my fate
Or is it Satan's trickery?
O merciful God above
Please help me understand,
Am I condemned to Hell
Or will I die and live
Again with You: in the
Paradise of Your love.
I've walked the narrow path;
Surely I'll go to Heaven.
Please God, end my doubt,
Will I go to Heaven,
Or must I go to Hell?
For ten years I've lived a
Life of abstinence,

Thinking only of Your words,
And should I live a hundred,
I'd spend them all in prayer,
Spend them all in praise of You,
This is my promise, Lord.
My life is serving You,
And if I fulfil this pledge
What will be my fate?
I cry to You in terror,
Answer this simple plea,
Will I go to Heaven above,
Or must I burn in Hell?   LxQ6 finishs

SCENE FOUR

Enter the Devil.   LxQ7

Paulo and the Devil.

THE DEVIL: For ten years I've battled
              For the soul of this hermit,
              Tempting him with pleasures,
              Taunting him with memories.
              Till now he stood as firmly
              Against all my trickery
              As this mountain stands firm
              Against the wind and rain.
              But today he has moved.
              My dream shook his faith,
              You heard his doubting words,
              Heard him doubt salvation.
              Christian faith is loving God
              Knowing that after death
              Is eternal life in Heaven.
              Paulo, who'd be a saint,
              Doubted his God's grace,
              Doubted his God's mercy,
              You heard his faithless question,
              You heard him beg to know
              That he wouldn't go to Hell.
              The root of his sin is Pride.
              Pride feeds his doubting heart;

I recognise the wound.
Pride was my falling sin,
For I am God's other son,
Lucifer, the brightest one.
When the hermit doubted Grace,
God gave me licence
To test his faith again.
To conjure more illusions.
How will he resist me,
This proud young hermit,
Who has tasted despair.
How will he resist me,
As I go down to him
Disguised as an angel.
I will visit Paulo
With a baited answer
To his faithless question,
And if he believes me
I'll drag him down to Hell.

SCENE FIVE

Paulo and the Devil.

PAULO: Master, I need an answer:
              Will I live with you in death?
              Will I know salvation?
              Please speak to your disciple.

THE DEVIL: God hears your question, hermit.
              He sees your streaming tears.

PAULO: *(Aside)* I'm overwhelmed with fear.

THE DEVIL: I've come to help you, hermit
              To resolve your confusion.
              That dream was an illusion,
              A device of the Devil.
              God wants you to know the
              End of your life's journey,
              The secret of your destiny.
              Please listen carefully.
              You must travel to Naples

                    And wait at the famous
                    Gate of the Sea.

PAULO: What joy,
                    Oh I am blessed by God.

THE DEVIL: Where you will meet Enrico
                    The son of Anareto.
                    Please listen to me closely.
                    He is a young nobleman,
                    Tall and elegant; enough.
                    I can tell you no more.
                    Enrico will be
                    The first man you meet
                    At the Gate of the Sea

PAULO: And when I see this man
                    What must I ask of him?

THE DEVIL: You shall ask him nothing.

PAULO: What then shall I do?

THE DEVIL: Observe him in silence,
                    Study all his actions.

PAULO: Angel of God, forgive me.
                    But fear blinds my heart.
                    Is this all I must do?

THE DEVIL: Paulo, be at peace.

PAULO: Amen.
                    I must watch in silence.

THE DEVIL: That is the will of God.
                    For it is written, Paulo
                    Your destiny is Enrico's,
                    The fate of his soul at death
                    Is the fate of your soul also.

                    The Devil goes.

PAULO: A miracle, a miracle,
                    A divine holy mystery.
                    I'll travel to Naples now
                    And wait for my Enrico,
                    My spiritual twin brother.

Who can doubt that Enrico
Is the holiest of men.

SCENE SIX

Enter Pedrisco.

PEDRISCO: *(Aside)* So, hunger wins again.
I've swallowed every blade,
And now comes indigestion.

PAULO: Pedrisco.

PEDRISCO: That's my cue.
Father, I'm at your service.

PAULO: We must make a journey.

PEDRISCO: *(Aside)* I want to leap into the
Air and scream with joy, Father.
Does our journey have an end?

PAULO: In Naples.

PEDRISCO: *(Aside)* Naples!
I can't believe my luck.
Tell me, Reverend Father,
What leads us to that city?

PAULO: As we walk, I'll tell you.
The story of a miracle
Which, if it be God's will,
Shall find its end in Naples.

PEDRISCO: As Naples was our home,
We might be recognised.

PAULO: We'll travel in disguise.

PEDRISCO: *(Aside)* As we've been gone ten years,
There won't be any problem.
When I was last in Naples,
Ten minutes was enough
For a man to forget
His best friend, his children,
And his wife.

PAULO: We must go.

PEDRISCO: May God protect us, Father,
                And guide us on our journey.

PAULO: *(Aside)* Joy wells up in my heart.
                Thank you for this gift, my Lord,
                I go to find Enrico
                And fulfil your holy will.
                How I long to know him,
                Enrico, chosen by you
                To be my holy brother.
                I've never known such bliss.

PEDRISCO: Father, I'll follow you.

                    Exit Paulo.

                This is a miracle, and
                I'm going straight to Juan's
                Where they grill the finest prawns,
                And then I'm off to see
                Marianna, the sexiest
                One-eyed landlady in Naples.

SCENE SEVEN

The Devil alone.   LXQ's 9, 10, 11

THE DEVIL: How faithfully I'm followed
                By the man who worships God.
                How earnestly he swallowed
                Both the bait and the hook.
                He wants to know his fate, well
                As he listens to Enrico,
                He'll create his own damnation.

SCENE EIGHT

The courtyard of Celia's house in Naples.   LXQ13

Enter Lizardo and Octavio.

LIZARDO: I must see this face, her
            Name is in every mouth.

OCTAVIO: What stories have you heard?

LIZARDO: That she is at once
            The most beautiful and
            Intelligent woman
            Who ever lived within
            The walls of this kingdom.

OCTAVIO: You have heard the truth.
            But Lizardo beware,
            For she uses her gifts
            As a trap, a sweet trap
            Which has snapped shut around
            The legs of a thousand
            Wealthy young visitors.
            She's a shrewd huntress
            Who smiles, flirts and pouts whilst
            Writing suggestive verses
            And accepting expensive toys.
            She seduces her suitors
            With sweet looks and poetry.
            Her poor victims pay her
            For the sonnets which she
            Composes in their honour;
            While they compete with one
            Another, praising her prosody,
            Her metrical ingenuity,
            Some even write themselves.

LIZARDO: She becomes more attractive
            With every word of warning.

OCTAVIO: This house is a brothel.
            The only pleasure is verbal.
            A whorehouse of poetry,
            Which welcomes customers
            From Germany, England,
            Hungary, Armenia, India,
            Italy, and even Spain.

LIZARDO: I can't believe . . .

OCTAVIO: It's true!
                  Are you still besotted?

LIZARDO: Every story I hear
                  Makes me want her more,
                  She sounds so exotic.

OCTAVIO: Something else you must know.

LIZARDO: You're a loyal friend.

OCTAVIO: She has one admirer
                  Who is as dangerous
                  As she is beautiful.

LIZARDO: You mean Enrico?

OCTAVIO: Yes.

LIZARDO: He has a reputation.

OCTAVIO: Naples never bred a man
                  So violent and immoral.
                  He lives to gamble and
                  When he's lost all his money
                  He comes here to visit
                  And relieves the lady of every
                  Expensive token which
                  She's charmed from her suitors.
                  If she tries to resist,
                  He knocks her to the ground.

LIZARDO: Poor lady!

OCTAVIO: Lizardo,
                  Your sympathy is touching,
                  But beware of this woman,
                  She won't strike your face,
                  But she might pick your pocket.

LIZARDO: Armed with your warnings,
                  I'll present myself to her.

OCTAVIO: I'm coming in with you.
                  Guard that purse, my friend.

LIZARDO: What shall we say to her?

OCTAVIO: Her weaknesses are greed,
                  And vanity. She thrives

On gold and flattery.
So, say you need a poetess
To compose you a love note.
Say that in exchange for
A few lines of rhyming verse,
You'll pay through the nose.

LIZARDO: Brilliant. And you?

OCTAVIO: I'll say
Something very similar.

LIZARDO: And here she comes, my friend.

OCTAVIO: If Enrico arrives
Whilst we're with her,
God in Heaven help us.

LIZARDO: He's only a man.

OCTAVIO: Possibly.

LIZARDO: Enrico is a criminal.
He's not worthy of our
Respect or our fear.

SCENE NINE

Enter Celia and Lidora.   L×Q 14

CELIA: A literate love letter!

LIDORA: Severino is intelligent.

CELIA: When?

LIDORA: You just praised his letter.

CELIA: I said it was literate.
His spelling is faultless,
His grammar correct and
His sentence structure sound.

LIDORA: I see. You mean he writes
Like a schoolteacher?

CELIA: Yes.
With all the passion of

| | A dictionary. God save me |
| | From tortured intellectuals. |

OCTAVIO: Lizardo, seize your moment.

LIZARDO: By God, she's handsome!
              The beauty of an angel,
              And the tongue of the Devil.

LIDORA: Madam, don't look now, but
              Your courtyard is graced with
              The uninvited presence
              Of two young noblemen,
              Neither of whom are poor,
              To judge by their clothes.

CELIA: I wonder what they want.

LIDORA: I wonder.

OCTAVIO: That smile's aimed at you.

CELIA: How may I be of service
              To your noble lordships?

LIZARDO: Forgive our intrusion,
              We felt free to enter
              Your courtyard, milady,
              Confident in the belief
              That the door of a poet
              Would not be shut against
              A patron, or a lover.

              Pause.

LIDORA: *(Aside)* My lady has the patience
              Of Job when awaiting praise.
              She won't say a word now
              Until he compares her
              To Calderon, Shakespeare
              Or Lope de Vega.

LIZARDO: Reports of your talent
              Have led me to your door.
              Madam, it is said by
              Those who speak of poetry,
              That your skill with words
              Is unequalled in the history

Of European literature.
You're more famous than Ovid,
Let alone Calderon,
Shakespeare or even the
Great Lope de Vega.
And so I come to beg
That you employ your skill
And bring some consolation
To a wounded heart.
I was loved by a lady;
She lived for my embrace
Until her cruel father
Forced her into marriage
With a rich old uncle.
If you could compose a
Few lines of lyric verse,
I would be pleased to reward
Your labours with a simple
Gift, and my humble heart.

LIDORA: *(Aside)* His "humble" heart, he says.
Rotten, would be my choice.

OCTAVIO: I come, my lady, with
A very similar request.

CELIA: Then speak.

OCTAVIO: I fell in love
With a beautiful woman,
Who returned my love while
There was money in my purse.
When my credit was spent,
She promptly disappeared.

LIDORA: *(Aside)* And who can blame the lady?

CELIA: Your arrival is fortuitous.
I was about to reply
To this letter from an
Intellectual admirer.
So, gentlemen, let me
Enrich your entertainment
By performing a feat
More audacious than Ovid
Could even dream of.

I shall compose three poems
Simultaneously.
Lidora, ink and paper.

LIZARDO: What dexterity!

OCTAVIO: An honour.

LIDORA: Gentlemen, ink and paper.

CELIA: Three, sonnets, I think.

LIZARDO: My pen is poised, my lady.

CELIA: Yours is to a woman
Forced into marriage?

LIZARDO: Yes.

CELIA: And yours is for a lady
With greed in her heart?

OCTAVIO: Yes.

CELIA: And I must reply to
Dear Señor Severino.

SCENE TEN

Enter Enrico and Galvan.

ENRICO: Are you looking for something,
Gentlemen?

LIZARDO: No, sir, no.
The gate was open . . .

ENRICO: Do you
Know who I am?

LIZARDO: . . . And so we
Came into the courtyard.

ENRICO: Well, you'd better get out.
Or by Christ Almighty,
If I lose my temper –
Celia, don't wink at me.

OCTAVIO: *(Aside)* Lizardo, please, back down.

ENRICO: I'll throw you into the sea.

CELIA: Enrico, if you love . . .

ENRICO: Don't you dare speak to me.
You, and you, get out fast.
Or by God above us,
I'll cut you both in half.

OCTAVIO: If we're not welcome here,
Then we'll leave at once.

LIZARDO: Are you this lady's cousin?
Her husband or her brother?

ENRICO: No. I'm the Devil.

GALVAN: And I'm the Devil's mate.
Let's cut them up.

OCTAVIO: Please, no.

CELIA: Enrico, in God's name . . .

OCTAVIO: Sir, we came here to ask
The lady if she would
Compose something on our behalf.

ENRICO: You wear fancy clothes,
But you can't write a letter?

OCTAVIO: Please, sir, don't be angry.

ENRICO: Who said I was angry?
What's this about writing?

OCTAVIO: Here, sir, look, this is all.

Enrico rips up the papers.

ENRICO: The poetry shop is shut.

CELIA: You ripped up all my . . .

ENRICO: Yes.
And don't push me or . . .

CELIA: Darling!

ENRICO: I'll rip up their faces.

LIZARDO: That, sir, is quite enough.

ENRICO: Look, I do what I do,
               And I get what I want,
               And if you get in my way,
               I'll break both your arms.
               So, noble sir, go home.
               When I tell you to go.

LIZARDO: I will not be treated
               Like a common lackey
               By a criminal.

OCTAVIO: Shut up, Lizardo!

ENRICO: Those are
               The words of a man, sir,
               So despite your lovely clothes,
               And affected manner,
               Which made me think you women,
               You must draw your swords, and
               Defend those fighting words
               With steel.

                    He draws his sword.

CELIA: Oh, Enrico!

ENRICO: Get out of my way!

CELIA: Stop fighting!

ENRICO: Celia,
               Heaven couldn't stop me now!

CELIA: Why am I cursed with him?

SCENE ELEVEN

ENRICO: Study our nobility.
               It runs better than it fights.

GALVAN: A perfect thrust!

ENRICO: Cowards!
               Let them take writing lessons
               In someone else's house.

CELIA: Enrico, are you hurt?

ENRICO: I put this point between
            The tall one's noble ribs,
            And slashed the velvet legs
            Of his brave friend with this.

LIDORA: *(Aside to Celia)* Our reputation
            For hospitality,
            Will be greatly increased.

GALVAN: I cut the small one's neck
            So the blood would run
            All over his silly ruff.

ENRICO: This is not the first time
            I've found strange men here.

CELIA: Please calm down, my love.

ENRICO: I don't like young idiots
            Visiting this house,
            Parading in front of you
            With their perfumed hair and
            Velvet doublet and hose.
            When they've finished paying
            Their barbers and their tailors,
            There's nothing left for you
            To charm out of their pockets.
            So why do you let them in?
            The next would-be suitor
            Who comes here to see you
            For poetry lessons
            Will meet an ugly end.

CELIA: I understand.

ENRICO: Good. Kiss me.

CELIA: Listen, Enrico,
            Those men may be foolish,
            But they're not poor fools,
            Look at this ring and chain.
            They may lack courage but
            They are not short of cash.

ENRICO: This chain's pure gold.

CELIA: It's yours.

ENRICO: And this stone is diamond.

LIDORA: Leave my lady something.

ENRICO: Celia, you seem to have
            Grown another tongue.
            Or was that you, servant?

GALVAN: Lidora, you could put
            That tongue to better use.

LIDORA: *(Aside)* Ooh, my clever mistress,
            She's fallen for the Devil,
            Who's served by a lizard.

CELIA: Take both the ring and chain,
            But let me speak, my love.

ENRICO: Speak.

CELIA: I want you to take me
            To the Gate of the Sea.

ENRICO: We'll go this afternoon.
            Wear the dress I gave you.

CELIA: I'll bring some food and wine.

ENRICO: Galvan, listen to me.
            Go and tell Escalante,
            Roldan and Cherinos
            That we're going with Celia
            To the Gate of the Sea.

GALVAN: Sure.

ENRICO: Tell them to meet us there.

LIDORA: *(Aside)* I'm looking forward to this.

GALVAN: And I'll take Lidora.

LIDORA: *(Aside)* My happiness is complete.

CELIA: Shall I wear my veil?

ENRICO: No.
            I want all Naples to see
            That you are my woman.

CELIA: I am your servant, sir.

LIDORA: *(Aside to Celia)* Those jewels are expensive,
            You gave in without a fight.

CELIA: It's a wise investment.

GALVAN: *(Aside to Enrico.)* What about the contract
            We're supposed to complete
            By seven o'clock tonight?
            Boss, we'll lose the money.

ENRICO: We've had half in advance.
            I spent it all last week.

GALVAN: Can we afford to go
            For a picnic by the sea?

ENRICO: I don't feel like working
            Now I've got this jewellery.
            We'll get the other half
            When the body's delivered;
            Murder doesn't take long.

GALVAN: So we'll kill him later?

ENRICO: Yes, and while I'm gambling
            The man who's got to die
            Will live a little longer.
            So, it's a work of charity.
            Even the Devil can preach.

SCENE TWELVE

Enter Paulo and Pedrisco.

PEDRISCO: You spoke to an angel?
            Father, you're blessed by God.

PAULO: It is a blessing, brother.
            A mysterious, holy gift.

PEDRISCO: You're twins in the spirit,
            Who will share the same fate?

PAULO: That was His holy word.
            If Enrico is damned,
            Then I'm damned also.

16 Pedrusco's Naples

And if his soul's saved,
Then I'll be saved with him.

PEDRISCO: He must be a holy man.

PAULO: I believe he must be.

PEDRISCO: Here is the Gate of the Sea.

PAULO: And here I'll wait for him.
The angel said he'd come.

Pause.

PEDRISCO: Above that whitewashed inn,
Lived a fat Spanish chef.
Born in Valencia.
I was his best customer.
And just across the way,
Lived a very tall girl,
With blond plaited hair,
And thick muscular legs.
Some said she'd been a soldier.
Others thought she was a man.
Anyway, it was certain that
My friend, the chef, was . . .

PAULO: Oh, Satan, my enemy!
He's tempting me with sinful
Thoughts of my past life.
Brother, listen to me.

PEDRISCO: Yes, Father.

PAULO: The Devil.
Taunts me with evil,
Memories of darkness,
Sick pleasures of the flesh.
(Paulo throws himself down to the ground.)
Come, brother, come, you must . . .

PEDRISCO: Oh dear! What's happening?

PAULO: I throw down my body
So that you can tread it.
Come, brother, come, you must
Stamp, stamp out wickedness!
Save me from temptation.

PEDRISCO :   Willingly, my father.
             (He stamps.)
             Am I doing this right?

PAULO :   Yes, brother.

PEDRISCO :   Does it hurt?

PAULO :   You must tread harder, brother.
             Pay no heed to my pain.

PEDRISCO :   I shall pay no heed at all.
             I'll tread and tread again.
             (Aside) I wonder if he'll burst?

PAULO :   Tread, brother, tread me hard.

ROLDAN :   *(Off)* Enrico, don't do it.

ENRICO :   *(Off)* I'll punish the bastard.
             He's going into the sea.

PAULO :   Someone said "Enrico".

ENRICO :   *(Off)* Why did God curse the world
             With beggars?

CHERINOS :   *(Off)* Don't kill him.

ENRICO :   *(Off)* And how will you stop me?

CELIA :   *(Off)* Please, one of you stop him.

ENRICO :   *(Off)* None of them would dare.
             I'm doing him a favour.
             (Enrico throws beggar off a cliff into the sea.)
             His poverty is cured.

ROLDAN :   *(Off)* My God, he's thrown him off.

SCENE THIRTEEN

Enter Celia, Lidora, Galvan, Roldan, Escalante, Cherinos.

ENRICO :   It makes me angry to see
             A man without pride. So,
             I rescued him from shame.

	I put him in the sea, Now he won't suffer, pity.
PAULO:	*(Aside to Pedrisco.)* He's murdered a poor man.
ENRICO:	His poverty is cured.
PEDRISCO:	*(Aside)* Maybe he'd begged too much. I wonder what he was asking.
CELIA:	That was cruel . . .
ENRICO:	Shut up or I'll fill your lungs with water.
ESCALANTE:	Enrico, let's forget it.
PAULO:	*(Aside to Pedrisco.)* He called him Enrico.
PEDRISCO:	Father, I know this man Is not your Enrico. This man is the Devil. Let's see what he does next.
ENRICO:	So, everyone, sit down. We've got something to discuss.
ESCALANTE:	Right, boss, let's sit and talk.
ENRICO:	Celia, you sit here.
CELIA:	I'm sitting.
ESCALANTE:	And you, my dear Lidora, sit by me.
LIDORA:	That will be a pleasure. Señor Escalante.
CHERINOS:	And you sit here, Roldan.
ROLDAN:	Here I am, Cherinos.
PEDRISCO:	*(Aside)* What a congregation! Father, if we move closer, We'll hear them much better.
PAULO:	*(Aside)* Where is my Enrico?
PEDRISCO:	Let's watch and say nothing. In these clothes we could be Mistaken for beggars, so . . .

ENRICO: I want us all to tell
               The story of our lives,
               Including every crime,
               The murders, thefts, rapes,
               Stabbings, robberies, and frauds.
               I want to hear them all.
               And the man whose story
               Tells of most wickedness,
               Evil and depravity,
               Will win a crown of roses.
               Have songs written for him,
               And sung to him whilst
               Bottles of wines are
               Poured down his throat.

ESCALANTE: That sounds like a fine way
               To spend the afternoon.

ENRICO: So, Señor Escalante,
               You must tell your story.

PAULO: (Aside) God stop their evil mouths!

PEDRISCO: (Aside to Paulo.) He is as bad as the boss.

ESCALANTE: Right!

PEDRISCO: Look at his evil smile.

ESCALANTE: I've broken into more
               Than twenty-odd houses.
               I've stabbed thirty policemen,
               Killing about half of them.
               I've robbed six banks and
               Sent fourteen men
               To their graves, for cash.

PEDRISCO: (Aside) I hope I live to see you
               Dancing in mid-air
               On the end of a rope.

ENRICO: Cherinos, you must speak.

PEDRISCO: (Aside) What a bad name for him.
               He's no Cherinos.

CHERINOS: I've never killed a man
               But I've stabbed hundreds.

ENRICO: You've never killed a man,
                So you're still a virgin.

CHERINOS: I don't know what saved them.
                The best scam I ever worked
                Was with a tailor who
                Made expensive clothes.
                He tipped me off when he'd
                Sold a very smart cloak,
                Told me the owner's name,
                And of course the address,
                So then I'd steal it back.

ENRICO: And he'd sell it again?

CHERINOS: Yes, after I took my fee.

ENRICO: Weren't the cloaks recognised?

CHERINOS: No. He'd recut the cloth
                Into waistcoats or hats.

ENRICO: Anything else, Cherinos?

CHERINOS: Not that I remember.

PEDRISCO: (Aside) This is like confession.
                Father, look at him.
                He's giving absolution.

CELIA: And now your story, boss.

ENRICO: I'm waiting for silence.

ESCALANTE: No lies, please, Enrico.

ENRICO: I only speak the truth.

GALVAN: Sure.

PEDRISCO: Father, come and listen.

PAULO: I'm waiting for Enrico.

ENRICO: So listen to my story.

CELIA: No one interrupt him.

PEDRISCO: (Aside) Listen to the sermon.

ENRICO: I was born to be evil,
                As my story will reveal.

18
Enzo's
Story

I grew up here in Naples,
Son of a rich merchant,
You all know my old father,
He was born a commoner,
He earned the title rich man,
Which has always seemed to me
The most useful decoration.
As a child I stole
My father's hard-won fortune
I stole coins from his purse
And later sold the purses.
I discovered the secret places
Where he kept his money and
I stole it all, every penny.
Then I made my first friends,
The dice, the card table and
The wheel: gambling became
My life, and gambling
Is the father of all crime.
I quickly lost the money
I'd stolen from my father,
So I turned to burglary.
I broke into people's homes,
Taking anything of value,
And went straight back to the dice,
The card table and the wheel,
Where I lost the money
I'd made from my robberies.
So then I joined a gang
Of specialist thieves who
Shared my love of gambling.
We did about fifty homes,
Killing six men in the process.
We worked as a team,
Dividing everything equally
We made together, and
We all went straight back to the
Dice, the cards, and the wheel.
One night the police chased us,
They caught everyone but me,
And despite being tortured,
No one gave my name.
As I watched them in the square,

Each one swinging on a rope,
I decided to work alone.
I learnt to stand outside
The gambling house at night,
Waiting for the winners,
From whom I begged. And, as they
Reached into their pockets,
I reached for my dagger
And buried it deeply
Between their unsuspecting ribs.
So, what they'd quickly won inside
They quickly lost again to me.
I started mugging women,
They're easier to overcome;
I threatened them with a blade,
And if they didn't yield,
I'd slash their lovely faces.
That's how I spent my youth;
Now I'll tell you of the man.
For all my adult life,
This sword's been my best friend,
Between us we've stopped the lives
Of thirty unlucky souls.
Ten I killed for nothing,
I mean I didn't get paid.
I killed the rest for money.
I've killed for one gold coin,
Which might sound a little cheap,
But I swear before you all,
When I'm short of money,
I'll kill for the price of
A drink, or a game of cards.
I've raped six poor virgins,
Which is lucky I suppose,
Its hard to meet one virgin,
In these dark sad times.
I wasn't so lucky one night,
When I broke into a house,
To make love to a woman
Who was married to a banker.
She woke up in her bed and
Screamed, I wasn't invited.
Her husband appeared waving

A sword and shouting insults.
I punched him in the face, picked
Him up with his grey hair
And threw him off the balcony,
Which was three floors up.
The bitch got hysterical,
So I razored her breasts,
Five times, or maybe six.
And as rivers of blood flooded
The meadow of her belly,
I watched her soul fly away.
I often do evil things,
For no good reason; I pick fights
With complete strangers, I killed
A man who was my friend,
Because I didn't like the way
He laughed at a joke.
I was in Rome one day when
A priest tried to save my soul.
I knocked him to the ground,
And kicked him into that
Better world he talked about.
Once I was organising
Protection for some people
Who owned little shops.
One of the businessmen
Refused to pay his dues,
So I had to go after him.
He ran away, I chased him,
He took refuge in a school,
The teachers locked the doors
So I couldn't get at him.
I set fire to the place and
Everyone was burned to death.
All the children turned to ash.
I enjoy offending God,
I've never been to Mass,
Never confessed my sins.
I hate the poor and needy,
I've watched men die of hunger,
While my purse was full of gold.
I've no fear of the law,
I've killed so many policemen,

They've stopped trying to arrest me.
I'm beyond their jurisdiction.
My final and worst crime
Is that I love this woman.
Her eyes are the only jail
Which can hold me prisoner.
But when I'm short of money,
I take all her earnings,
And leave her with nothing.
I take her money, and go
To see my father, you all
Know old Anareto.
He lives alone in poverty,
For five years he's suffered
Some incurable affliction,
He's crippled, he can hardly walk.
He sits at home waiting for
Me to turn up with some food.
I blame myself for his ills,
He's never recovered from
Losing all his money to the
Dice, the cards and the wheel.
Everything I've said is true,
I swear by Jesus Christ.
So, judges, what's the verdict?
Who deserves the prize?

PEDRISCO: *(Aside)* He missed his vocation.
             He's a politician.

ESCALANTE: You deserve the crown.

ROLDAN: And the songs.

CHERINOS: And the wine.

CELIA: Here's your crown of roses.

ENRICO: May you live for ever.

                    Celia crowns Enrico. They kiss.

CELIA: And now, let's eat.

GALVAN: And drink.

CELIA: Long live my Enrico.

ALL:	Long live Enrico, Son of Anareto.
PAULO:	*(Aside)* Oh Heaven forgive me.
ENRICO:	Let's go down to the sea.

SCENE FOURTEEN

Paulo and Pedrisco.

PAULO:	Stream, my tears, stream And break, my heart, break. Let no sense of shame Stop you drenching the earth With bloody drops of grief.
PEDRISCO:	What's the matter, Father?
PAULO:	Oh, cursed and rejected, I am damned to Hell. That was my Enrico.
PEDRISCO:	Father, that can't be true.
PAULO:	He bears all the marks.
PEDRISCO:	And what does that mean?
PAULO:	That was my Enrico, The son of Anareto. I heard him speak both names.
PEDRISCO:	That man will burn in Hell.
PAULO:	This was my secret fear. If Enrico is damned, Then Paulo is damned. The angel spoke God's word. Oh, I am damned to Hell. How can God forgive that man? One who has burnt children, One who brags of raping, He is beyond God's mercy.
PEDRISCO:	Father, I'm sure you're right.

PAULO: Oh, my divine Master,
                Why have You punished
                Me so cruelly?
                I've lived in Your service
                For ten years on a mountain,
                Eating only bitter grass
                And drinking river water.
                I've been so devoted,
                Hoping that on Judgement Day
                You would lift me up
                I thought I'd be saved and
                Now I see You're sending
                Me to burn in Hell.
                You've been so hard on me,
                I can already feel the flames
                Melting the flesh off my bones.

PEDRISCO: Patience is a virtue!

PAULO: How can I be patient,
                Knowing what I know.
                Who can be silent when
                He knows he'll go to Hell,
                To be tortured and burnt
                Until the end of time.
                To always, always be
                In pain, pain without end.

PEDRISCO: (Aside) I'm getting frightened now.
                Father, why don't we just
                Go back to the mountain?

PAULO: We'll go back, Pedrisco,
                But not to do penance!
                God said if he went up
                Then I'd go up with him,
                And if he went down,
                I'd join him. So be it.
                Since I must share his death,
                I can share his life as well.
                God forgive my anger, but
                If Enrico's death is mine,
                His life will be my guide.
                Is it just that he should live
                A life of wild pleasures,

PAULO: Whilst I live with nothing and
Yet we both go to Hell?

PEDRISCO: No, Father, it's not just.

PAULO: We'll live on the mountain!
Not fasting and praying,
But looting and killing.
No longer as holy men,
Now we are bandits.
I'll follow Enrico,
Just as cruel, just as selfish,
I'll be worse if I can.

PEDRISCO: YES, Father, let's do it.
Throw down your old rags;
Rip off your crucifix,
Let's go and buy some clothes.

PAULO: I'll terrorise mankind!

PEDRISCO: But what about money?

PAULO: I'll steal from nunneries!

PEDRISCO: So, Father; Paulo, let's go.

PAULO: Lord pardon my revenge,
If it seems excessive,
But You have condemned me,
You spoke the word which
Can never be broken.
I'm going to enjoy
My life on earth as I
Know I'm going to Hell.
I'll live as a criminal,
Lord, I am Enrico!

Exit Paulo.

PEDRISCO: I'll follow my master,
And become a bandit.
I wonder if I'll have
To follow him to Hell?

END OF ACT ONE

44

ACT TWO

SCENE ONE

20 Gambling

Galvan and Enrico.

ENRICO: Gambling, you're killing me!
Go back to the Devil
And take all his money.

GALVAN: Enrico, you never win.

ENRICO: You hands, burn, burn in hell.
How could you throw away
So much money?

GALVAN: The game's fixed,
It's always fixed, loaded dice.

ENRICO: Galvan, today I was
Using my own loaded dice.

GALVAN: Boss, gambling is for fools.

ENRICO: These hands will destroy me.
They've just tossed away
A chain and a diamond ring.

GALVAN: Easy come, easy go.
You've got them for nothing
Let's not mourn their passing.

ENRICO: Lost, with two simple throws.
Have you ever known a man
Who always, always lost.

GALVAN: Get out of this mood, boss.
Laura's brother's paying us
To kill Albano, and as
You've spent his down payment
And lost the jewellery
We'd better do the job.

ENRICO: My purse is empty, so,
I'll have to kill Albano.

GALVAN: And please, boss, don't forget
            You have an appointment
            Later with Cherinos
            And Escalante.

ENRICO: Sure,
            They're doing Octavio's place,
            The rich Geonovese, right?
            (Aside) I'm a balcony-climber;
            If you're going to steal
            From the rich you need a
            Good head for heights, and this
            Is the best in Naples.
            So bring them here, Galvan.

GALVAN: I'm going, boss. It's good to
            See you back in business.

SCENE TWO

Enrico alone.

ENRICO: They'll wait for night to
            Wrap itself around the streets,
            Before they risk coming out.
            So, time to see my father.
            He lives behind this door.
            For five years he's lived here,
            All that time I've paid his rent,
            And for five long years,
            He hasn't walked a step.
            And for all those years
            He's had no one but me.
            All the money that doesn't
            Get thrown away on cards,
            Or dice, or drinking gets
            Spent looking after him.
            In all my evil life,
            I've only had one virtue,
            Only one of God's laws
            I've piously obeyed,
            "THOU MUST HONOUR THY FATHER"

Although I stole his money,
I've never disobeyed him.
And he doesn't know I'm
The one who stole his fortune.
In fact, he doesn't know
About any of my crimes.
Because, although I've
Hardened my heart against
The tears of many victims,
One tear of disappointment,
Falling from his eye
Would stop me living out
This cruel life I love.

2.2
Anareto's
house

SCENE THREE

Anareto and Enrico.

Anareto asleep in a chair.

ENRICO: Here is my father
            Fast asleep in his chair.

ANARETO: Enrico, my dear son

ENRICO: Please forgive me, I'm late.

ANARETO: My son, you're never late.

ENRICO: I don't mean to hurt you.

ANARETO: I'm happy just to see you.

ENRICO: The joy felt by the Earth,
            When the sun warms its soil
            And turns its clouds red,
            Is nothing compared to
            The joy which warms my heart
            When I see you, dear Father.
            My days are dark and cold,
            You bring me warmth and light.

ANARETO: Son, goodness lives in your heart.

ENRICO: Well, have you eaten?

ANARETO:	No.
ENRICO:	You must be hungry, Father.
ANARETO:	You are my nourishment.
ENRICO:	Those are kind words, Father. But you speak from your love And not from your belly. It's four in the afternoon, Time for us to eat. I'll get the table ready.
ANARETO:	Thank you, my Enrico.
ENRICO:	Father, this is my duty. *(Aside)* I sold the jewellery For a thousand gold coins. I hid one from myself, Safe in a back pocket, So I could feed my father, Whilst the rest of the gold Fed the hungry dice. Here's some bread, eat.
ANARETO:	God thank you for this, son. Oh Lord, look upon him, He is my hands and arms.
ENRICO:	Please, you must eat your bread.
ANARETO:	My fingers can't rip the loaf.
ENRICO:	Let me help you, Father.
ANARETO:	Your arms give me strength.
ENRICO:	If only this embrace, Could give you new life. Father, this illness is A kind of living death.
ANARETO:	"Thy will, not mine, be done."
ENRICO:	Your food is on the table, I can carry you over.
ANARETO:	I'm tired . . .
ENRICO:	But the food . . . well, sleep.

ANARETO: It's cold.

ENRICO: Let me put this
            Blanket on your shoulders.

ANARETO: That's better, son.

ENRICO: And now, sleep.

ANARETO: There's only one thing I'd like
            To see before I die.

ENRICO: What?

ANARETO: Your wedding day.

ENRICO: I'll get married tomorrow.
            (Aside) I'm not getting married,
            I only spoke those words,
            To make him feel better.
            They might be the last words
            My father ever hears.

ANARETO: To witness your wedding,
            Would give me new life.

ENRICO: Oh, you'll live for ever, Father.

ANARETO: Then I should die contented.

ENRICO: Father, I'll get married . . .

ANARETO: Let me give you some advice.
            Don't marry for beauty,
            A pretty wife is a curse;
            For such a woman will be
            Offered a thousand temptations,
            And human beings are weak . . .
            Listen, Enrico . . .

ENRICO: Speak on.

ANARETO: Never doubt your wife's love,
            For a jealous husband creates
            The crime that he so fears.
            A wife is no more and
            No less than her husband.
            You must love her and serve her
            All the days of your life.
            So marry a good woman,

> And always, always, trust her.
> Don't doubt her in anything,
> For doubt breeds doubt, and when
> You tell her you love her . . .

He falls asleep.

ENRICO: Sleep stops his wise old tongue,
          Just as the lesson's ending.
          I'll wrap him up tightly,
          And settle him for sleep.

SCENE FOUR

Enter Galvan.

GALVAN: Enrico, we're ready.
          Albano's coming.

ENRICO: Who?

GALVAN: Albano, the dead man.

ENRICO: What?

GALVAN: The old man we've got to kill.

ENRICO: Why should I kill him?

GALVAN: Are you afraid?

ENRICO: Galvan,
          I'm afraid to open
          These tired old eyes,
          With the noise of murder.

GALVAN: Who is this old man?

ENRICO: The only man I respect.
          The wisest, bravest man,
          The only man I fear.
          Every son must love
          And fear his father.
          If we were always as
          Close as we are now,
          I'd never commit another
          Ugly crime, for his eyes

Would stop my cruel hand.
Galvan, close the door
So I can't see his face,
Every line and wrinkle
Drains away my strength.
Close the door, now, quickly,
Or I'll be defeated,
Won over to pity.

GALVAN: The door's closed.

ENRICO: Thank you.
I can get on with my work.
And what's the job, murder?
You watch me, Galvan,
I'll murder Naples.

GALVAN: Look, Albano's coming.
He just turned the corner.
Laura's brother will be
Getting impatient.

ENRICO: So,
He walks down his last street.
Let the gravemaker start
Digging up his earth.

GALVAN: Murder doesn't take too long.

SCENE FIVE

Enter Albano, crossing the stage.

ALBANO: Every night I walk out
To watch the setting sun.
Soon the sun will be
Watching my life end.

         He exits.

ENRICO: I can't move.

GALVAN: What's happening?

ENRICO: This Albano is the
Living portrait of the

Man I most honour,
the man I most love.
If I kill Albano,
I'll be killing my father.
Albano, you can carry on
With your evening strolls.
Your white hair's stopped
Me cutting your throat.
My honour, (oh yes, even
I dare speak of honour)
My honour, will not let me,
Stain those white hairs red.

GALVAN: Boss, what's happening?
            These aren't the actions
            Of the great Enrico!

ENRICO: I am still Enrico.

GALVAN: We could have done the job.

ENRICO: Listen to me, Galvan:
            I've commited murder,
            And never been afraid.
            I've set fire to houses,
            And laughed at burnt bodies.
            But when I see white hairs,
            I will not do evil.
            To honour my father
            I pardoned Albano.
            I show old men respect.
            And if I'd known Albano,
            Was the image of my father,
            I'd never have agreed
            To take his old life.

GALVAN: Well,
            This is strange respect.
            Laura's brother will expect
            Us to pay back the money,
            Which you've already spent.
            We can forget about
            The other half as all
            Old men seem to live under
            Your special protection.

ENRICO: Maybe!

GALVAN: Maybe?

ENRICO: Laura's brother,
                Can ask me for his gold.

GALVAN: And here he is, right on cue.
                He won't need prompting,
                When asking for his money.

SCENE SIX

Enter Octavio.

OCTAVIO: I've just seen Albano
                On his evening walk;
                He shows no sign of dying.

ENRICO: Albano must live, Sir.

OCTAVIO: You promised to kill him
                And I gave you money.
                You swore on your honour.

GALVAN: *(Aside)* This one won't last long.
                Look, the boss is fingering
                The hilt of his sword.
                You always know what's coming
                When he gets itchy fingers.

ENRICO: I don't murder old men.
                If you want him dead,
                You can kill him yourself.
                I've spent all your gold.

OCTAVIO: Return my money, Sir!

ENRICO: You, go, and go quickly!
                Or by Christ Almighty
                I'll cut you in half.

                A big fight begins.

GALVAN: *(Aside)* This will wake up Satan.

OCTAVIO: I want my gold!

ENRICO: Here's some steel!

OCTAVIO: You're a cheat, and a coward.

ENRICO: And you're a lying fool.
                (Enrico stabs Octavio.)
                A dead, lying fool.

OCTAVIO: Will I die now?

ENRICO: Soon.

GALVAN: *(Aside)* If he'd gone home without
                Asking for his money back,
                He'd be lying in his bed.
                Instead, he's lying here,
                Dying in a pool of blood.

ENRICO: I kill vain fools like you,
                Not wise old men who
                Bless us with their wisdom.

<u>SCENE SEVEN</u>

26
the Militia

The sound of officers of the law and the Governor of Naples.

THE
GOVERNOR: *(Off)* I want him taken alive,
                But if he resists, kill him.

GALVAN: Boss, it's really bad news.
                The Governor of Naples,
                With an armed militia.

ENRICO: Let them send an army.
                My options are simple;
                If they take me alive
                I'll be hanged in the square.
                But if I put up a fight,
                Then maybe I'll escape.
                If it's my time to die,
                Then I'll die with honour
                With a sword in both hands.

OFFICER 1:   *(Off)* Here is Enrico.

OFFICER 2:	*(Off)* Cowards, advance.
GALVAN:	We're surrounded.
ENRICO:	Jesus Christ,
	Let them stand where they will,
	I've got two sharp swords,
	I'll hack them in pieces.
GALVAN:	Boss, I'm right behind you.
ENRICO:	I'm not a man, I'm Satan!

Enter the Governor of Naples and the militia; huge fight ensues. Enrico hacks people to death.

THE GOVERNOR:	You're the Devil, Enrico.
ENRICO:	I'm fighting for my life.
THE GOVERNOR:	Surrender your sword.
ENRICO:	I'll never surrender.

What remains of the militia, runs away. The Governor tries to arrest Enrico. Enrico mortally wounds the Governor and then he and Galvan beat a hasty retreat.

THE GOVERNOR:	I'm hurt.
OFFICER 3:	Oh my God!
OFFICER 1:	He's killed the Governor!
OFFICER 2:	May Heaven protect us!

SCENE EIGHT

On a cliff, at the edge of the sea.

Enter Galvan and Enrico.

ENRICO:	If the Earth opened and hid me in darkness,
	They'd dig me up and drag me from her arms.
	After killing him, there's nowhere to hide.
	I'll have to jump into this dangerous sea.
	And You, great Judge above us, hear my prayer:

Though I've lived an evil, sinful life,
I've never doubted Your wisdom and grace.
But how can I jump into this graveyard?
I can't leave my father to fend for himself.
Oh Anareto, poor crippled old man,
I'd like to carry you high above the waves,
Like Aeneas, carrying old Anchises.

GALVAN: Boss, don't jump!

ENRICO: Come with me!

GALVAN: We'll be killed on the rocks.

ENRICO: Forgive me, dear Father,
For although I can't carry
You away in my arms,
I swear that I carry
Your image in my heart.
Follow me when I jump.

GALVAN: Boss, I'm right behind you.

ENRICO: We can't escape by land.

GALVAN: I'll jump!

ENRICO: We'll jump down
Into the sea's dark centre,
Best tomb for a murderer's bones.
Oh my beloved father,
This is a painful farewell.
And Heaven as I can't help
Him any more, I entrust
Him to Your special care.

Growing sound of pursuing militia.

GALVAN: Shall I jump first, Boss?

ENRICO: Galvan, we'll go together!

They jump into the sea.

SCENE NINE

The forest on the mountain. Paulo and Pedrisco dressed as bandits, with a gang of other bandits, and three prisoners.

BANDIT 1:   Master, what's the decision,
              Do they live, or do they die?

PAULO: Have they given everything?

PEDRISCO: They didn't GIVE a penny.

PAULO: So what's the delay, fools!

PEDRISCO: We TOOK all their money.

PAULO: They offered resistance?
              Then the decision is simple.

PEDRISCO: What do we do, Master?

PRISONER 1:   Please, spare our lives.

PAULO: Hang them!

PRISONER 2:   Mercy, Sir!

PAULO: From the oak!

PEDRISCO: Come on, you'll be fine fruit.
              You'll weigh down the branches
              And fatten up the birds.

PAULO: Do I shock you, Pedrisco?

PEDRISCO: Master, only yesterday
              You stood on this mountain,
              Outside a humble cave,
              Begging God to bless you
              With the gift of grace so
              That you might continue
              Your life of meditation,
              Penitence and prayer.
              And today you're a bandit,
              The vicious leader of
              A gang of desperados,
              Who ambush travellers,
              Steal their possessions
              And hang them from trees which
              Grow on the very same
              Mountainside where you lived
              The life of a holy man.
              So, yes, of course I'm shocked.
              I'm so shocked I don't think

Anything will ever
Shock me again.

PAULO: Enrico
Is my inspiration.
As we must die together,
Bound to the same cruel fate,
It is right that I should
Imitate his actions.
And God forgive me if
I offend you in this,
But I promise to be
A fiercer criminal than
Enrico, that's justice!

PEDRISCO: I don't doubt that you know
Exactly what you're doing.

PAULO: Oh why did that angel
Fall down from Heaven
Through the crystal spheres
And speak those words which
Have driven me from grace?
And why should the man
Who gave his life to God,
Who lived like a saint,
Be rewarded like this?

PEDRISCO: There's no answer, Master.

PAULO: You beasts, who make your homes
On this wild mountainside,
Witness my revenge,
More cruel than nature,
More reckless than Phaeton.
And beware you trees,
Whose leaves protect the Earth,
For beneath your green canopy,
I'll murder and rape.
And whilst you give fruit
To feed hungry mankind,
I'll use men to feed birds.
I'll hang a severed head
From every tree, and my fruit
Will ripen in winter,

	Spring, and summer, an Eternal crop of blood.
PEDRISCO:	*(Aside)* He's going to Hell in style.
PAULO:	You, go and hang our guests.
PEDRISCO:	Like the wind I go.
PRISONER 1:	Please, spare . . .
PAULO:	Don't speak a word or I'll Have your throat cut out.
PEDRISCO:	Come on.
PRISONER 2:	I'm terrified.
PEDRISCO:	*(Aside)* I play the executioner, The worst job in the gang. I bet when we get caught, I'll have to teach the hangman How to tie the knot and push.

SCENE TEN

Paulo and two bandits.

PAULO:	Enrico, hear my prayer: As I must join you in death, I swear to live your life, So I'll always be with you. And on that terrible day When we are judged We'll have given God Good cause to send us To burn eternally in Hell. *(Voice off, singing.)*
THE VOICE:	God's greatest gift is mercy, So no man despair. For all may be forgiven However great the crime.

PAULO: Who is that singing?

BANDIT 1:   I can't see for the trees.
              (Voice off, singing.)

THE VOICE: If a man repents
              All of his earthly sins,
              Then God in his mercy,
              Will surely forgive him.

PAULO: You two, go up the mountain
              And bring me that singer.

BANDIT 2:   Yes, Master.

PAULO: Quickly, then.

              The two bandits exit.

VOICE OFF: *(Singing)* The great King of Heaven,
              Speaks to all sinners
              Offering salvation
              To each and every one.

<u>SCENE ELEVEN</u>

Enter a shepherd, weaving a crown of flowers.

PAULO: Come down, young shepherd.
              Who taught you that song?
              Every word you sang found
              An echo in my heart.

SHEPHERD: God taught me my song.

PAULO: God?

SHEPHERD: Yes, through the Church,
              His wife on Earth.

PAULO: Blessed be
              His Holy Church.

SHEPHERD: Amen.
              I love God with all my
              Heart and soul and mind.

I obey all His laws,
Every commandment.

PAULO: Do you believe that God
Could forgive a man who
Had sinned against Him
In thought, word and deed,
Who'd broken all His laws?

SHEPHERD: Yes, if a man says to God
"Oh Father, I have sinned",
Then, let his offences
Be as numberless as
The stars in the sky,
God will forgive them all.
Let him but speak the words,
"Father, forgive me for
I have sinned," and God's arms
Will open to embrace him,
And surround him with love.

PAULO: Wait, shepherd, don't go yet.

SHEPHERD: Sir, I must leave you for
I am searching the mountain
For a ewe lamb that's lost.
She strayed from my master's
Flock and I must find her.

PAULO: What are you making?

SHEPHERD: A crown of flowers, Sir,
For the lamb when she's found.
My Master bid me do this
For he loves her dearly,
As he loves all his flock.
If a man offends God,
Let him ask forgiveness,
For He is all mercy
And He is all love.

PAULO: Wait, shepherd.

SHEPHERD: I cannot.

PAULO: I'll keep you by force.

SHEPHERD: It would be much easier,
                To stop the sun in its course.

SCENE TWELVE

Paulo alone.

PAULO: I've forgotten God's mercy.
          That shepherd just warned me
          That I've made God angry
          By doubting His mercy,
          In my sinful despair.
          All his parables
          Embody one lesson,
          Every one of his stories,
          Tell one simple truth,
          If a man shall repent,
          Then God will forgive him.
          So Enrico may repent
          And God may forgive him,
          Forgive all his sins
          And take him to Heaven.
          Paulo, you are making
          A terrible mistake,
          But this savage criminal
          Is known to all as the most
          Evil man in the world.
          How can he be forgiven?
          Shepherd, if you can see me,
          Understand my confusion.
          If Enrico intends
          To offer repentance,
          Then all my suffering
          Has been a delusion.
          Oh shepherd, do you believe
          That Enrico will repent?
          And do you believe he
          Deserves holy mercy?
          There's only one answer,
          To all of these questions,
          Enrico is irredeemable,
          And both of us are damned.

SCENE THIRTEEN

Enter Pedrisco.

PEDRISCO: Master, please listen hard
To what I must tell you.
Though you won't believe it,
Every word is true.
You may think I'm crazy
Or making up stories,
But I tell you it happened.
So believe what I say.
Celio and I set off
To hang the three travellers
From the oak tree which grows
Right over the cliff's edge.
You know the place I mean:
Where the mighty waves
Hurl themselves hard against
The broken rocks and the
Spray cuts into your face.
Well, just as we'd suspended
Our unlucky victims,
From their picturesque gibbet,
We heard a mighty scream,
Coming up out of the sea,
"I'm drowning," said the voice,
And so we looked down into
The wild sea where we saw
Two bouncing wet faces.
One was biting a sword.
Well, the sea was so angry,
She hurled the bodies high,
And then dropped them down hard
Against sharp, pointed rocks,
So that blood stained the foam.
The wind whipped the waves
Into high pointed spikes
Which seemed to support two
Decapitated heads.
And so, without mentioning
My great personal bravery

And heroic sacrifices,
I'll tell you quickly without
Wasting any more precious words,
That both men are rescued,
And one of the saved men
Is your Enrico!

PAULO: You're right, I don't believe you.

PEDRISCO: You must believe, Master,
              I just saw it all happen.

PAULO: You saw my Enrico.

PEDRISCO: Yes, Master, with both eyes.

PAULO: And what did he do when
              He knew he'd been saved?

PEDRISCO: He said,
              "Jesus Christ Almighty".

PAULO: (Aside) Shepherd, do you still believe
              That God could forgive him?
              But as he's arrived here
              I'll settle my confusion
              With an experiment
              Which will quickly reveal
              His spiritual intentions.

PEDRISCO: He's being marched this way.

PAULO: Pedrisco, come with me,
              Listen to my instructions.

SCENE FOURTEEN

*Enter Enrico and Galvan, soaking wet, with their hands bound, led by
Paulo's bandits.*

ENRICO: Where are you taking me?

BANDIT 1:   Our Master will answer.

PAULO: (Aside to Pedrisco.)
              Can you do that?

PEDRISCO: Yes, Master.

BANDIT 2:   Is the boss going?

PEDRISCO: Oh yes.
             Where were you going when we
             Pulled you out of danger?
             Trying to walk on water?
             Well, why don't you answer?
             Where were you going?

ENRICO: To Hell!

PEDRISCO: Why take such a painful route?

ENRICO: Stop wasting my time.

PEDRISCO: Brave words, friend, tell me
             What's your name?

ENRICO: Satan.

PEDRISCO: Is that why you like water?
             Some relief from the fire?
             Well, where do you come from?

ENRICO: If the sea had not
             Ripped my sword from my teeth,
             I'd give a quick reply
             To your stupid questions
             By cutting your throat.

PEDRISCO: Please, friend, don't start shouting.
             If you threaten me again,
             I swear to God I'll stab
             This blade through your heart.
             Just remember you're my
             Prisoner, and if you think
             You're brave, I tell you,
             I'm as brave as Hector.
             And if you think yourself
             The only vicious killer
             I'll tell you I've murdered
             Quite a number of dinners.

BANDIT 1:   That's enough, Pedrisco.

ENRICO: (Aside) Why do I have to listen
             To this?

PEDRISCO: Tie him to a tree.

ENRICO: I won't try to resist.

PEDRISCO: And his friend.

GALVAN: *(Aside)* It's all over.

PEDRISCO: *(To Galvan.)*
               Your face tells the story
               Of a hard, nasty life.
               Bring them here and bind them.
               (To Enrico.)
               Move towards that tree, Sir.

ENRICO: This is my reward from God.

              Enrico and Galvan are tied to separate trees.

PEDRISCO: Now you.

GALVAN: Have pity on me.

PEDRISCO: Blindfold them.

GALVAN: *(Aside)* I'm going to die.
               Listen to me, bandits,
               We all share the same trade;
               Don't murder a brother.
               I'm a criminal like you.

PEDRISCO: I want to save the hangman
               A difficult job.

BANDIT 1:   Their hands are bound tight
               And they can't see a thing.

PEDRISCO: So load up your bows, boys,
               And fill our friends with bolts;
               Two dozen in each one.

BANDIT 1:   Ready.

PEDRISCO: *(Aside)* No one must shoot,
               The Master's instructions.

BANDIT 1:   Does the boss know these two?

PEDRISCO: Come on, we've got to leave.

SCENE FIFTEEN

Enrico and Galvan, alone, tied to a tree.

GALVAN: They'll kill us.

ENRICO: Don't break
            In front of these fools.

GALVAN: Boss,
            I can already feel
            The arrows in my belly.

ENRICO: This is God's justice,
            I'm being punished
            For my evil life,
            I want to beg forgiveness,
            But the words won't come.

SCENE SIXTEEN

Enter Paulo, as a hermit, with a cross and rosary.

PAULO: I've conceived this trick
            To test Enrico.
            To see if he'll repent
            At the moment of death,
            And beg God for mercy.

ENRICO: *(Aside)* I never thought I'd die
            Alone in the wilderness.

GALVAN: *(Aside)* I think every mosquito
            Is a sharp arrow
            Flying straight at my head.

ENRICO: *(Aside)* Fortune, why have you brought
            Me here to die,
            Tied to a barren tree
            And shot to death by fools?

PAULO: May the Lord God be praised!

ENRICO: May He be praised for ever.

PAULO: May God give you courage
            To bear this unhappy blow.

ENRICO: Who is it who speaks of God?

PAULO: A holy man who lives
            Here on the mountainside,
            Who knows that you'll die soon,
            Murdered by bandits.

ENRICO: What do you want with us?

PAULO: I've begged a few moments
            From those who will kill you.
            I'm here to help you die.

ENRICO: How can you help me die?

PAULO: I'm offering you confession.

ENRICO: Father, save your breath.

PAULO: Are you a Christian?

ENRICO: Yes.

PAULO: Then accept absolution.
            Why do you refuse
            The final sacrament?

ENRICO: Because I don't want it.

PAULO: *(Aside)* Oh God, it's as I feared.
            You know they'll kill you

ENRICO: This is my last request,
            Let me die in silence.
            And, bandits, if you're going
            To kill me, do it now.

PAULO: *(Aside)* My heart is breaking.

ENRICO: I'll never surrender.

PAULO: Surrender to God.

ENRICO: God knows all my sins,
            Why should I remind him?

PAULO: *(Aside)* Godless blasphemy.

Because His sacred love
Will redeem all your sins.

ENRICO: Look, I'm no hypocrite.
I've never been to church,
It's too late to start now.

PAULO: *(Aside)* His heart is made of stone.

ENRICO: Galvan, what do you imagine
Celia's doing now?

GALVAN: How can you think of her
When we're going to die?

PAULO: Don't think of such things.

ENRICO: Don't make me angry.

PAULO: Are you angry at the name
Of God?

ENRICO: Leave me alone,
Father, because if I
Get this rope off my hands,
I'll kick you in the sea.

PAULO: Remember, death is near!

ENRICO: Let it come, and welcome.

GALVAN: Father, confess me.
I'm terrified of dying.

ENRICO: Father, if you want to help,
Then take off my blindfold.

PAULO: Certainly, my son.

ENRICO: Thank God that I can look
Upon the world once more.

GALVAN: Please, take off my blindfold!

PAULO: Certainly, my son, but
It will only reveal
The faces of your murderers.

SCENE SEVENTEEN

Pedrisco and the bandits return, armed with crossbows.

ENRICO: So why are you waiting?

PEDRISCO: Make your confession.

ENRICO: I don't want to confess.

PEDRISCO: Celio, you fire first.

PAULO: Please let me speak again.

PEDRISCO: Take aim.

PAULO: Don't kill them yet.
            (Aside) Oh why won't he repent?
            If he dies in this state,
            He'll go straight to Hell,
            And I'll have to follow.

ENRICO: Cowards, I order you,
            Put those bolts in my body.

PEDRISCO: This time we won't wait!

PAULO: Wait!
            (Aside) What will happen if he dies?
            My son, confess your sins.

ENRICO: Yes, I'm a sinner.

PAULO: Beg God for salvation.

ENRICO: Father, you bore me.

PAULO: *(Aside)* Oh I can't stop my tears.
            Now I know I've lost Heaven,
            Now I know I've lost God.
            I must take off these robes,
            I can't dress in sacred black.
            I'm like a snake who sheds,
            No, not a snake, for when
            He casts away his skin,
            He throws away dead flesh,
            Whilst I discard a robe,
            Which is the uniform of God.
            I'll re-assume the Devil's

Clothes and play the bandit.
As I remove this cloth,
It seems to speak to me.
"Paulo, hang me on a tree
You were never worthy."
So give me my sword again,
And buckle on my dagger,
Take away my crucifix,
I'm a stranger to redemption.
Untie their hands.

ENRICO: Freedom!
Hermit, what's going on?

GALVAN: Bend your knee and thank God
For sparing both our lives.

ENRICO: Hermit, I want to know
What's happening.

PAULO: Enrico,
You are my damnation:
I wish that Heaven had
Killed you in the womb or
Your nurse had smothered you
Whilst you lay in your cot.
I wish that Heaven had
Thrown you from a balcony
When you were a young man,
I wish that you'd been killed
As you raped and robbed,
Murdered and blasphemed,
For you've destroyed my life,
Destroyed my hope of heaven.

ENRICO: I don't understand.

PAULO: Listen to my story.
My name is Paulo
And once I was a hermit.
I left home as a young man
To live the holy life
And in a cave near this place
I spent ten years of my life
In prayer and meditation.

ENRICO: A pure life.

PAULO: A cursed life.
            I was shaken by a dream
            And begged God for help.
            An angel came down to me
            And spoke these awful words,
            "Paulo, go to Naples
            And look for Enrico,
            The son of Anareto.
            Watch all his deeds.
            And listen to his words.
            If he goes to Heaven,
            Then you'll go to Heaven.
            And if he goes to Hell,
            Then you'll go as well."
            "Oh, Enrico is my brother,
            Enrico is a saint."
            These were my joyous words
            As I set off for Naples.
            But when I reached the town,
            I saw you kill a beggar
            And heard you tell an
            Evil story, the story
            Of your life in crime.
            You rejoiced in every word,
            You showed no remorse.
            So, certain that you'd be damned,
            I abandoned my holy life
            And became a criminal.
            These men are my followers,
            We also rob and murder,
            As I must share your fate,
            I will also share your life.
            When the sea washed you up,
            I took my chance to test
            Your faith to see if you
            Would repent your sins,
            To see if you'd make confession.
            Now all my hope is gone,
            You failed my test, so
            Both of us are damned.
            I've thrown away those robes

And taken up this costume
Because I'm going to Hell,
Because that's what God wants.

ENRICO: If God had sent an angel,
He wouldn't speak so clearly,
God is not so simple.
Heaven speaks in riddles.
You shouldn't have left your life
Of prayer and meditation.
If you've committed any sin,
Then that's the real one.
You became a criminal
To take revenge on God.
And you doubted His mercy,
But He's not cut you down.
So perhaps what He seeks
Is your soul's salvation.
I am the worst of men,
But still I hope for mercy.
I've never been to church
Unless it was to steal.
Never been to confession,
Though I've plenty to confess.
Never thought much of God
Or His Holy Mother.
But when you held that sword,
Hard against my throat,
I never doubted God,
Never doubted I'd be saved.
There's no logic to my faith,
I've never done good work,
Never prayed, but I know,
That God will save me,
I know that he loves me.
Paulo, if you want to
Live here on this mountain,
Let's join up our forces
And live our lives together.
I can't go back to Naples,
And if God damns me then
We'll live and die together
But I have more faith

In His love and pity
Than His sword of justice.

PAULO: That's some consolation.

GALVAN: *(Aside)* What's Enrico saying?

PAULO: You must rest, come with me.

ENRICO: Oh, my Father: my friend,
            There is a jewel in Naples
            Which I can't leave behind.
            So though I fear the danger,
            I must go back to the city
            And retrieve my precious one.
            I'll take one of your men.

PAULO: Please, take Pedrisco,
            He's brave and loyal.

PEDRISCO: *(Aside)* It's a difficult choice
            But I think I'd prefer
            To go to Naples
            With Enrico rather
            Than carry on as a bandit.

PAULO: Enrico, take my sword.
            Give them our best horses,
            You'll be there in two hours.
            They run like the wind.

GALVAN: I'll stay here, and do jobs.

PEDRISCO: And I'll go to Naples,
            Where, no doubt, I'll be whipped
            For all the other jobs
            You've done, Galvan.

ENRICO: Goodbye,
            Paulo, my dear friend.

PAULO: The name begs an embrace.

ENRICO: Paulo, I'm a sinner,
            But God will save my soul.

PAULO: Enrico, we're damned!

ENRICO: Despair will damn you.

PAULO: No, I'm damned whatever.
                Oh, Enrico, I wish
                That you'd never been born.

ENRICO: I know I'll go to Heaven;
                God gave me that hope.

ACT THREE

SCENE ONE

32
Prison

Enrico and Pedrisco in prison, in Naples.

PEDRISCO: I'm glad I came with you!

ENRICO: Why are you complaining?

PEDRISCO: Because I'm in prison
For someone else's crimes!

ENRICO: You're alive!

PEDRISCO: Not for long!
I'll die of starvation
Before they can hang me!

ENRICO: We get three meals a day.

PEDRISCO: Can you eat the food?

ENRICO: Stop!
That's enough! Just endure!

PEDRISCO: I'm so hungry.

ENRICO: Shut it!

PEDRISCO: I've lived such a good life –
Ten years of abstinence.
Why should I pay the price
For Galvan's petty crimes?

ENRICO: Pedrisco, be quiet.

PEDRISCO: Enrico, I'm silent . . . *(Pause)*
Oh, but who can resist
The power of hunger!
It opens every mouth.

ENRICO: Have faith; we'll escape.

PEDRISCO: Yes, I'm sure we'll make an exit . . .

ENRICO: Then why are you afraid?

PEDRISCO: From this world to the next!

ENRICO: Have no fear.

PEDRISCO: Enrico,
               I dreamt of two men
               Dancing in silence with
               Both feet off the ground.

ENRICO: I'm dancing with Lady Luck.

33.
Celia's entrance

SCENE TWO

Enter Celia and Lidora.

CELIA: Lidora, I'd like you
               To enter before me!

LIDORA: My lady, as your servant
               I don't have any choice.

ENRICO: I can hear Celia!

PEDRISCO: Who is this Celia?

ENRICO: A woman who loves me
               With all her heart and soul.
               Soon we'll be free.

PEDRISCO: *(Aside)* Oh yes,
               But will we be fed?

ENRICO: She'll be carrying money
               So we can bribe the guards.
               We'll need somewhere to hide it,
               Have you got a bag?

PEDRISCO: Er . . . No!
               (Aside) But as my belly's empty
               I'm feeling quite inventive,
               I'll tie knots in my shirt,
               And . . . there, a sack!

ENRICO: It's small.

PEDRISCO: It's not that small, why are
               We arguing over a shirt?

               Enter Celia and Lidora.

34 Eunzo +
Celia
Meet.

ENRICO: Celia, my angel!

CELIA: *(Aside to Lidora.)* He calls me his angel,
            Lidora, I'm lost!
            (To Enrico.)
            Enrico, dear sir.

PEDRISCO: "Dear sir"?
            Politeness is frightening.

ENRICO: Kind, loving, Celia . . .

CELIA: Are you well, Enrico?

ENRICO: Healed by your presence.
            I've longed to see your eyes.

CELIA: Enrico, I must give . . .

PEDRISCO: Yes! Oh what a woman;
            GIVE is the best of words.
            The bag is wide open,
            I hope the knots hold fast.

ENRICO: So, what can you give me?

CELIA: Everything.

ENRICO: *(To Pedrisco.)* I told you.

PEDRISCO: Fortune smiles upon us!

CELIA: The Judge has decided
            You both deserve to die,
            They'll hang you tomorrow!

PEDRISCO: *(Aside)* That news has filled my sack.

ENRICO: Celia, listen to me.

PEDRISCO: *(Aside)* No room for any more.

CELIA: Enrico, I'm married.

ENRICO: Married, oh Jesus Christ!

PEDRISCO: Don't start insulting him,
            We'll need his help tomorrow.

ENRICO: Who dared to marry you?

CELIA: Lizardo.

ENRICO: I'll kill him!

CELIA:	No, I'm very happy.
ENRICO:	I'll cut him in pieces.
CELIA:	Please, make peace with Heaven. Tomorrow, you will die.
LIDORA:	Celia, come away.
ENRICO:	Celia, I'm dying.
CELIA:	I've got to go now.
PEDRISCO:	*(Aside)* God, This is really funny.
CELIA:	I know that you want me To have Mass said for you, I'll do it Enrico, and May Heaven protect you.
ENRICO:	Oh Heaven melt these bars.
LIDORA:	Celia, don't listen, You must come away now.
ENRICO:	Was any woman so cold, So faithless and cruel?
PEDRISCO:	*(Aside)* Time to put my shirt on.
CELIA:	Your soul is in danger.
ENRICO:	I can't think of danger, I'm so full of anger. *(Exeunt Lidora and Celia.)* That woman is a whore.

SCENE THREE

PEDRISCO:	These coins are counterfeit, They hardly weigh an ounce.
ENRICO:	Why do I suffer this? I'll break these manacles And rip open those bars.
PEDRISCO:	Calm down!

ENRICO: Shut up, you fool.

PEDRISCO: Stop making so much noise.

ENRICO: Jesus Christ Almighty.
               I'll slaughter Lizardo.

PEDRISCO: The guards have come.

ENRICO: And welcome.

SCENE FOUR

Enter two guards.

GUARD 1:   Enrico's gone crazy.
               Let's civilise the beast.

ENRICO: I'll kill Celia first,
               Then I'll kill Lizardo,
               This chain is my weapon.

PEDRISCO: Control yourself.

GUARD 2:   Get him.

GUARD 1:   Kill the beast, kill him!

ENRICO: I'll destroy this prison,
               Jealousy inspires me.

               Big fight, Enrico chases guards off.

GUARD 2:   He caught me with the chain.

ENRICO: *(Returning)* Cowards!

PEDRISCO: You've killed this guard.

VOICES OFF,
GUARDS AND
PRISONERS: Kill him, bastard, murderer etc.

ENRICO: Now I don't need a sword –
               This chain is my weapon.
               Why do you run away?

PEDRISCO: Here comes the governor.

SCENE FIVE

Enter the Governor, gaolers and more guards.

THE
GOVERNOR: Stop that man, hold him down.

               Enrico is overpowered.

GUARD 1:   He's killed Fidelio.

THE
GOVERNOR: By Heaven, Enrico,
If the judge had not just
Ordered me to hang you,
I'd bury this sword
In your evil throat.

ENRICO: *(Aside)* God, must I endure this?
Fire pours from my eyes.
I have no respect for you
Or your office, Governor,
And if God released me now
I'd rip you in pieces and
Swallow every mouthful,
And even then my anger
Would not be satisfied.

THE
GOVERNOR: The rope will stop your mouth,
Put more chains on him.

ENRICO: As many as you like,
You'll never stop me.
I'm so deep in sin that
I've forgotten how to feel.

THE
GOVERNOR: Put him in the dark cell.

ENRICO: Governor, I'm the devil,
And the devil loves darkness.
Take me out of the light,
I hate all Heaven's gifts.

               They drag off Enrico.

PEDRISCO: Poor Enrico!

GUARD 1: Poor Fidelio!
That's his blood on the floor.

Everybody leaves. Pedrisco alone.

PEDRISCO: I'm sure it's dinner time.

VOICES OFF: Food's up, food's up!

PEDRISCO: At last!
This is my final chance
To swallow any food,
If it's too disgusting
I'll fill my shirt with gruel.
So when I get to Hell,
I can bribe the devils.
Pedrisco's no fool.

SCENE SIX   37 Stocks.

Enrico alone in a dark cell.

ENRICO: So now I find myself
Chained in a dark cell,
Waiting for the hangman
To come and stretch my neck.
Enrico, be brave and
Courage, don't desert me
When they come to kill me.
For stories must be told
About the death of Enrico,
They'll tell of my bravery
And celebrate . . . Who's there?

VOICE: Enrico . . .

ENRICO: Who calls me?
Oh Heaven, whose voice can
Breed such fear in my heart?

VOICE: Enrico . . .

ENRICO: It calls again.

VOICE: Enrico . . .

ENRICO: I've no strength,
I can't offer resistance.
Who can make me so afraid?
Perhaps it's a prisoner
Lying in the corner
Chained up to the wall
And left here to die.

SCENE SEVEN

The Devil and Enrico.

THE DEVIL: *(Invisible to Enrico.)*
I come to heal your fear.

ENRICO: I'm so shaken with fear
I don't know who I am.
My heart beats like a drum
Marching soldiers to battle.

THE DEVIL: I want you to be free.

ENRICO: But how can I trust you,
I don't know who you are.

THE DEVIL: Enrico, here I am!

                          The Devil appears as a shadow.

ENRICO: You have no substance,
All I see is a shadow.

THE DEVIL: Don't be afraid.

ENRICO: My veins
Are full of ice.

THE DEVIL: Enrico,
That name will be legend.

ENRICO: Please, stay away from me.

THE DEVIL: This is your final chance.

ENRICO: My heart will burst . . .

*The Devil makes a sign, and a door appears in the
prison wall.*

THE DEVIL: Do you see that door?

ENRICO: Yes.

THE DEVIL: Walk through it, Enrico,
It leads to freedom.

ENRICO: Who
Are you?

THE DEVIL: Walk through the door
And don't ask my name.
I am a prisoner,
I want you to be free.

ENRICO: *(Aside)* Shall I walk through the door?
If I stay I'll be hung
Yes, I'll out to freedom.
But my legs won't obey,
I can hear another voice.

VOICE 2: Enrico, you can't run.
Please stay in prison
It's the way to be free.

ENRICO: *(Aside)* I trust that sweet voice
I won't go through the door.

THE DEVIL: You fool, you've been tricked.
That voice is a phantom,
Created by your fear.

ENRICO: If I stay here I'll die.
I'm going through the door.

VOICE 2: Don't run from this prison;
For if you go, you'll die,
And if you stay, you'll live.

ENRICO: If I leave here I'll die,
But if I stay, I'll live?

THE DEVIL: Through the door is freedom.

ENRICO: It is better to stay.

THE DEVIL: Fear has destroyed you,

Stay in this cell and
Await execution.

SCENE EIGHT

Enrico alone.

ENRICO :   The shadow's disappeared,
              And I'm in confusion.
              Perhaps I should leave, but
              Now the door's disappeared.
              Was there a door here or
              Did I imagine it?
              I can't believe the fear
              That aches in my stomach.
              "If I leave here I'll die,"
              The sweet voice told me.
              But if I stay here, I'll hang,
              Of that I am certain.
              I don't know what to do.

SCENE NINE

Enter the Governor.

THE
GOVERNOR :   I'll see him alone, so
              You guards stay outside.
              Enrico . . .

ENRICO :   Who are you?

THE
GOVERNOR :   Summon all your courage,
              Listen to your sentence.

ENRICO :   Governor, please, speak on.

THE
GOVERNOR :   *(Aside)* I see no repentance.
              In the case of His Majesty's

Prosecutor-Fiscal against
The accused, Enrico, in this
Kingdom of Naples, we find
The accused guilty of murder,
Armed robbery, assault, rape,
And many other crimes.
He must be taken from this place
With a noose about his neck,
With a crier preceding him,
Reciting the list of his crimes.
He must be taken to the square
Where a gallows is erected
On which he will be hung by the neck.
And may no person take him down,
Without our licence and order.
This day . . . etc etc in the King's name!

ENRICO: Do I have to hear this!

THE
GOVERNOR: What did you say?

ENRICO: Listen, fool.
If you were worth killing,
I'd . . .

THE
GOVERNOR: Words will change nothing.
Think of your eternal soul,
Beg God for His mercy.

ENRICO: Did you come to save my soul
Or to read out my sentence?
Hypocrite, for God's sake
Get out before I kill you.

THE
GOVERNOR: Then die, and burn in Hell.

39 Stock B.

SCENE TEN

Enrico alone.

ENRICO: So, I'm sentenced to death.

I've got two hours left
Of this miserable life.
Oh voice of the air,
You said if I stayed here
I'd live, and if I ran
Away I'd die, well thank you
For your good advice.
Shadow, you offered freedom,
I should have listened to you.
My luck's gone, lost again.

40 Guard.

SCENE ELEVEN

Enter Guard 1.

GUARD 1:   Two Franciscan friars
            Have come to confess you.

ENRICO: Jesus Christ, that's funny.
            Tell the brothers to go home.

GUARD 1:   Think of your eternal soul.

ENRICO: I'll die and go to Hell,
            No one else will pay for
            The sins I've committed.

GUARD 1:   You're an evil bastard.

ENRICO: You've said enough, now go.
            Jesus Christ Almighty,
            If I lose my temper . . .

GUARD 1:   I've gone.

ENRICO: And none too soon.

41 Stocks 3

SCENE TWELVE

Enrico alone.

ENRICO: What will I say to God
            When he asks about my life?
            What can I say to him

When he asks about my sins?
To confess seems foolish;
Whose mind is large enough
To remember all those sins?
How could I recall all
The evil things I've done?
So let's forget confession,
I'll hope for God's mercy.
He pities all mankind,
He might still forgive me.

SCENE THIRTEEN

Enter Pedrisco.

PEDRISCO: Enrico, it's me again,
I've come to say goodbye.
And to remind you that
There are two monks out here.

ENRICO: Tell them to go away.

PEDRISCO: Aren't you afraid of Hell?

ENRICO: Christ, I'm getting angry.
I'll kill you and the monks
If you don't leave me alone.

PEDRISCO: They've come here to save you.

ENRICO: If you don't get out now,
I'll kick you through the walls.

PEDRISCO: I'd thank you for that.

ENRICO: Go away, Pedrisco.

PEDRISCO: Go to Hell, Enrico.
I hope they burn you slowly.

SCENE FOURTEEN

Enrico alone.

ENRICO: Oh you voice of the air,

You were sent by an enemy
Hungry for revenge.
You told me not to leave
The walls of this prison.
Your counsel was foolish,
Soon they will hang me.
Shadow, you pitied me.
You offered me freedom,
I was a coward,
I should have run away.
Come back now shadow,
And watch how I die.
I'll die like a hero
With dignity and courage,
I'll spit at the world.

SCENE FIFTEEN

Enter Anareto and Guard 1.

GUARD 1:   You speak to him, old man,
            Perhaps your silver hairs
            Will soften his hard heart.

ANARETO: Enrico, my dear son,
            It hurts me to see you
            Chained up in this cell,
            It hurt me to hear
            The truth of your life,
            All the evil you've done.
            But also I'm happy
            That you're being punished;
            For if you leave this life
            Having paid for your sins,
            Having truly repented,
            Then you'll leave this life
            In a state of grace; and
            The pains of this life are
            As nothing to the pains
            Which are suffered in Hell.

ENRICO: Oh Father . . .

ANARETO: Enrico,
          Can you call me father?

ENRICO: I don't understand . . .

ANARETO: If you will not know God,
          I can't call you my son.

ENRICO: Father, how can you say this . . .

ANARETO: If you will not know God,
          You're no longer my son.

ENRICO: I don't understand . . .

ANARETO: Enrico, Enrico . . .
          Today they will hang you,
          You must confess your sins.
          If you refuse to repent
          Then your soul will be lost.
          Your life's been a battle,
          A war against Heaven.
          To wage war on Heaven
          Is like fighting a mountain,
          When your fist hits the rock,
          Then your bones will splinter.
          If you're angry with God
          And you spit at Heaven,
          That which you've cast up
          Will fall back in your eye.
          The hangman is waiting,
          There is no escape now.
          So fall down on your knees
          And confess to Heaven
          All the sins of your life.
          Oh beg for salvation,
          For God is all mercy,
          And He will forgive you.
          So, if you are my son,
          Humble yourself to God,
          And if not, (Oh my tears),
          Then I will disown you.

ENRICO: Father, my dear, Father . . .
          You have touched my soul more
          Than any fears of hanging.

> I'll make my confession,
> And beg God for mercy.

ANARETO: Oh you are my son.

ENRICO: I'll
> Never disobey you.

ANARETO: Make your confession.

ENRICO: How I hate to leave you.

ANARETO: How I hate to lose you.
> We must go.

ENRICO: I'm going to die.
> I've lost all my courage.

ANARETO: There are no words.

ENRICO: Father . . .

ANARETO: Oh my son, oh my son . . .

ENRICO: Oh, merciful, almighty God,
> You who look down upon us from
> That fortress of light where you tread
> The shining hills of Heaven,
> Hear me, hear me, oh hear my prayer.
> I've been the worst of men to pass
> Through the light of this world, I've
> Committed more wrongs against you
> Than there are grains of sand in the sea.
> Lord, your love is stronger than sin.
> To redeem the suffering of Man
> You gave your only begotten Son,
> To die upon a cross of wood,
> Lord, may I be worthy to touch
> A single drop of that Holy Blood.
> And Mary, oh beauteous Virgin,
> Who lives surrounded by angels,
> Whose love is a shelter for sinners,
> Oh Mary, Mary, I have sinned,
> Pray for me, I beg, pray for me
> Now, at the hour of my need.
> Ask the fruit of Your womb, Jesus,
> To remember His life on Earth,
> To remember the suffering

Which He endured to save us.
And tell him that I wish now,
Now that I know and understand
That I would prefer to suffer
A thousand thousand deaths rather
Than to have offended Him once.

ANARETO: They're coming.

ENRICO: Lord have mercy,
Lord have mercy, Amen.

ANARETO: *(Aside)* That a father should see this . . .

ENRICO: And now I understand
The voice and the shadow.
The voice was an angel,
The shadow, the Devil.

ANARETO: Son, we must go.

ENRICO: Who can
Hear that name and not weep.
Please, stay with me, Father.

ANARETO: Yes, my son, till the end.

ENRICO: God is a sea of love.

ANARETO: Be brave.

ENRICO: I'll trust in Him.
We must go to the square.
Where I'll lose my life,
The life that you gave me.

SCENE SIXTEEN

Paulo alone in the forest.

PAULO: I'll settle here and sleep,
With grass for a pillow;
I'm so tired of living
The life of an outcast.
I'll sleep in the shadow
Of this hanging willow,

And hope no cruel dream
Reminds me of what's to come.
There's a river down there
At the bottom of the hill,
And as its strong current
Hits stone against water
A sound like music
Echoes through the trees.
You careless young river
Make me a happy song,
Make me a song which
Will take away memory.
And there in a birch tree
A finch sings out clearly,
Inspired by the river
To celebrate his lover.
Oh sing me a lullaby,
A lullaby of innocence,
A lullaby of freedom
So I can sleep away
All thoughts of what's to come.

SCENE SEVENTEEN

Enter the shepherd, undoing the crown of flowers.

SHEPHERD: Dark tangled forest
And cold clear river,
The shepherd has returned.
Come again to walk
Your narrow pathways
Come again to share
In your dark beauty.
I grazed my flock here,
I stood on this bank
Watching my sheep
Drink down your water.
And I was envied
By other watchmen
Because my master
Showed me such favour.

He showed me favour
As I was careful
Never to lose
Any one of his sheep.
But now my master
(Who lives far away)
Shows me no favour,
His precious one is lost.
Oh he hasn't smiled,
Since that day when
The best of his flock
Ran out of the fold.
Now I am unhappy,
All joy has left me,
I can't sing the songs
Which rang through these trees.
All I can sing now
Are pitiful dirges.
On this green hillside
I picked the blossoms
To build a flower crown
To adorn the neck
Of my stray ewe lamb,
When she came home.
But she stayed away,
Misled, full of pride,
Away she has stayed,
From he who loves her
And cares for her life.
Now I must unpick
This garland of flowers,
And cast the petals
Down into the river,
To wash away hope.
Now she'll never wear them.

PAULO: Hey, watchman, I've seen you
           Before on these mountains,
           Then you were anxious
           Because of a stray lamb.
           But I am amazed,
           You seem so unhappy.

SHEPHERD: Oh lamb, oh lost one,

What joy you run from,
What pain you run to.

PAULO: Isn't that the garland
               You were weaving when
               I last saw you?

SHEPHERD: Yes.
               This is her garland
               But she's gone away
               And will not return
               To the love that waits.
               So I must unpick this.

PAULO: But if she came back
               Would you accept her?

SHEPHERD: Yes.
               I would receive her,
               Although I'm angry.
               My master has told me
               That if she returns,
               I must embrace her,
               Even if she returns
               Blackened and dirty.
               I must welcome her,
               Surround her with love.

PAULO: You obey your master?

SHEPHERD: In all things. But she
               Won't answer my call.
               I've whistled her and
               Often tried to warn her.
               I've searched every day,
               Look at my feet sir
               They're cut and broken
               From walking on brambles,
               They're bloodied and sore,
               Pierced by sharp thorns.
               I have to stop searching.

PAULO: (Aside) Tears wash his young face.
               If she has forsaken you
               Then you must forget her.

SHEPHERD: Soon I must forget.

Return, you flowers,
Return to water.
She was not worthy
To carry your beauty.
Farewell, you forest,
I must go to my master
And tell the sad news,
He already knows.
But even as I tell him,
He'll weep once more.
I go towards him
Full of shame and fear.
For what he must say
Will hurt me, I know;
He'll say to me "Shepherd,
Is this how you care
For the life I gave,
Into your hands."
And I will say "Master,
I have no answer,
There are no words,
There are no words,
I can only weep,
I can only grieve."

Exit shepherd.

SCENE EIGHTEEN

Paulo alone.

PAULO: Is he telling my story?
           But why speak in riddles?
           If he wants to warn me,
           He should say so clearly.
           *(Heavenly music, bright light and two angels carrying
           Enrico to Heaven.)*
           I'm blinded by sunlight,
           And high in the air
           I can see two white angels
           Bearing a blessed soul
           Up into His kingdom,

Up into His glory.
Oh blessed, blessed soul,
Today you will be held
In God's loving hands.
The reward you deserve
For a life of goodness.
You flowers of the forest,
Witness this miracle,
Watch Heaven's curtain open,
Watch clouds parting,
And see that lucky soul
Rising up to happiness.
Rising up to be with God.
Sad the soul who fails
To receive this reward,
Sad the soul whose life
Has not deserved this gift.

47 the peasants are coming

SCENE NINETEEN

Enter Galvan, running.

GALVAN: Paulo, master, beware!
                 Marching down the mountainside
                 Is a well-drilled army
                 And it's us they're after.
                 I think we should run.

PAULO: An army?

GALVAN: If you listen
                 You can hear the drums beating;
                 And look on the horizon,
                 You can see the banners waving.
                 They'll kill us if they catch us.

PAULO: Who are they?

GALVAN: Peasants, sir.
                 Villagers and farmers.
                 They hate us for stealing
                 Their cattle, their women
                 And their money.

PAULO: I'll fight!

GALVAN: What!

PAULO: I'll slaughter them.

GALVAN: It's an army!

PAULO: And I'm Paulo!

GALVAN: We'll die.

PAULO: I'm a nobleman,
           Worth a thousand peasants.

GALVAN: Listen to the drums, master!

PAULO: Watch me draw my sword.
           Before I was a hermit,
           I'd served the King's army.

SCENE TWENTY

Enter an army of peasants, led by the Judge.

JUDGE: Today you'll be punished
           For all your evil crimes.

PAULO: My heart's on fire, so
           Come on you peasants, fight.
           I'm fiercer than Enrico.

PEASANTS: Surrender.

GALVAN: *(Aside)* I'm running.
           You can't fight an army.

           Galvan runs off, Paulo exits fighting peasants.

SCENE TWENTY-ONE

PAULO: *(Off)* Is this a sign of peasant courage,
           That you won't stand and fight me,
           But shower me with arrows?
           Two hundred fight one noble sword.

JUDGE: *(Off)* He's running down the mountain.

               Paulo enters, falling down the mountain, covered in blood, filled with arrows.

PAULO: My hands can't hold my sword,
               And my legs can't hold me up.
               I'll die in the mud, disgraced,
               Massacred by peasants.
               I can't be shamed like this,
               I'll get up again and . . .
               Oh, I can't move, I can't see,
               This is Heaven's revenge.

SCENE TWENTY-TWO

Enter Pedrisco, running, he doesn't notice Paulo.

PEDRISCO: I was found not guilty,
               So when they'd hung Enrico
               They kicked me out of town,
               And I've come back to find
               The mountainside in uproar.
               There's Fines, bleeding, with
               An arrow in his neck;
               And there's two big farmers
               Chasing Celio away,
               And here, oh God help me,
               My master, full of arrows.

PAULO: I'll kill you, peasant,
               I'm not dead, I can still . . .

PEDRISCO: Master, it's Pedrisco.

PAULO: Pedrisco, lift me up.

PEDRISCO: How did this happen, sir?

PAULO: Peasants, Pedrisco, peasants.
               Tell me about Enrico,
               What happened, Enrico?

PEDRISCO: They hung him in the square.

PAULO: So he's gone to Hell.

PEDRISCO: Be careful what you say,
            He died as a Christian,
            With prayers and confession
            He went to the gallows,
            Kissing a crucifix
            And chanting the rosary
            Begging God for mercy
            Whilst tears wet his face.
            When his neck was broken,
            Holy sound filled the square,
            Two angels appeared,
            Surrounded by pure light
            And they lifted his soul
            In glory to Heaven.

PAULO: Enrico's gone to Heaven!

PEDRISCO: Don't doubt God's mercy!

PAULO: You've been tricked, you fool.
            That was another soul,
            Enrico's gone to Hell.

PEDRISCO: *(Aside)* Dear God, you convince him.

PAULO: I'm dying . . .

PEDRISCO: Enrico
            Is held in God's arms
            Beg Heaven for forgiveness.

PAULO: How can God forgive me!

PEDRISCO: He forgave Enrico;
            Surrender to Heaven.

PAULO: God is mercy . . .

PEDRISCO: Amen!

PAULO: But God won't forgive me!
            Hold me, Pedrisco, oh . . .

PEDRISCO: Enrico's in Heaven,
            Try to end as he did.

PAULO: God made me a promise.
            If he goes to Heaven,

                    Then I go to heaven.
                    That was God's word.

                        He dies.

PEDRISCO: My master's dead; he died
                    Without seeing. The man
                    Who had faith has gone up
                    To Heaven. My master,
                    I think, will go to Hell,
                    Damned for despair.
                    I'll cover his remains
                    With branches of willow.
                    Oo, hello! Someone's coming.

SCENE TWENTY-THREE

Enter the Judge, peasants and Galvan.

THE JUDGE: If Paulo has escaped,
                Our efforts are wasted.

PEASANT: I saw him, full of arrows,
                Falling down the mountain.

THE JUDGE: Arrest him and bring him here.

PEDRISCO: *(Aside)* Unlucky Pedrisco,
                I can't escape this one.

PEASANT: This is one of Paulo's men.

GALVAN: Wrong, peasant, I only
                Ever served Enrico.

PEDRISCO: *(Aside)* Galvan, friend, help me.

THE JUDGE: Where is Paulo hiding?
                Tell us and you'll go free.
                Come on, speak up.

PEDRISCO: Don't shout,
                Shouting won't wake him up.

THE JUDGE: What do you mean?

PEDRISCO: He's dead!

I found his poor corpse,
Bleeding, full of arrows;
He's dead, he bled to death.

THE JUDGE: Where's the body?

PEDRISCO: Under here.

Paulo appears in flames.

PAULO: You need seek no further;
Fix your eyes on Paulo,
His body scorched by fire
And wrapped about with snakes!
I blame no one but myself,
I wanted to understand
The riddle of my destiny;
So I offended God
And the Devil took his chance,
Speaking many lies to me
In the shape of an angel.
But still I might have lived;
I doubted His mystery,
I had no faith in mercy.
Today God spoke to me,
"Down", said he, "You must go
Down, into the darkness,
There you'll be punished."
A thousand times I curse
My father and mother
For giving me life.
A thousand times I curse
Myself for doubting God,
For He is the sea of love.

GALVAN: Poor, unlucky Paulo.

PEDRISCO: And lucky Enrico;
He's gone to Heaven.

THE JUDGE: Free those men.

PEDRISCO: Thank you God!
Galvan, old friend, as
Neither of us has a boss,
What shall we do now?

GALVAN: I'LL LIVE A HOLY LIFE.

PEDRISCO: I don't suppose I'll live
             To see you canonised.

GALVAN: Have faith.

PEDRISCO: Yes, friend, I do.

THE JUDGE: We must go to Naples
             And tell this sad story.

PEDRISCO: If you find all this
             Too difficult to believe,
             Our author recommends
             That you read 'Belarmino'
             Or 'The Life of the Fathers'
             For all this did happen!
             It's recorded in those books.
             Kind jury, our story ends here,
             Heaven keep you safe.

                    THE END

DON GIL OF THE GREEN BREECHES

DON GIL OF THE GREEN BREECHES received its British première at the Gate Theatre, Notting Hill in December 1990. The cast was as follows:

DONA JUANA	Emma Richler
QUINTANA	Brian Lipson
CARAMANCHEL	Richard Hope
AGUILAR/DON ANTONIO	Martin Hyder
OSORIO/FABIO	Dave Roberts
DON MARTIN	Simon Kunz
DON PEDRO	Hugh Dickson
DONA INES	Kate Lock
DON JUAN	Simon Roberts
DONA CLARA	Vicki Pepperdine
VALDIVIESO/POLICEMAN	Peter Ryan
DON DIEGO	George Pounder
DIRECTOR	Laurence Boswell
DESIGNER	Ian MacNeil
COSTUME DESIGNER	Jessica Tyrwhitt
LIGHTING DESIGNER	Ace McCarron
MUSIC	Mick Sands
PRODUCER	Caroline Maude
DRAMATURG	Jon Bryant

ACT ONE

SCENE ONE

Segovia Bridge.

Dona Juana (dressed all in green as a man) and Quintana.

QUINTANA: Dona Juana, if we cross
The Segovia Bridge
We will enter Madrid.
Is that our destination?

I could cry in wonder
At the view while you seem
As sad as those little streams
Cutting through the slums.

Watching the Manzanares
Wash away the city's filth,
I'm trying to imagine
What misfortune brings us here.

Something must be very
Wrong to make my Lady
Put aside her dress and
Take to wearing breeches.

DONA JUANA: Quintana, please don't ask.

QUINTANA: I haven't said a word
Since last Monday morning
When you came to me in tears
And we left Valladolid.

As you begged me to not
Question what provoked our
Departure, here I am on
Friday, confused, near Madrid.

While I've followed along
Behind, you wouldn't believe
The explanations being
Considered in my mind.

Your sudden absence will

Have left your house desolate;
Think of your father, he must
Be getting desperate.

Tell me what's happening
And where you're taking me;
Surely my loyalty
Deserves some kind of answer.

You were so frantic when you
Came to me for help, I felt
I had to follow you.
I feared for your honour.

So rather than stay at home
To comfort my master,
I saw it my duty to
Protect that precious jewel.

I can't stay silent any
Longer; tell me the cause
Of all this unhappiness;
Please end my confusion.

DONA JUANA : It's not an easy confession.

QUINTANA :   Speak.

DONA JUANA :   Eight weeks ago it was
The Holy Feast of Easter,
When the fields of our dear
Valladolid were wearing their
April clothes of bright green silk.
I ran over the grass with
An innocent soul but I came
Home without one; it's still lost.

That was the day of the
Public opening of our
New bridge, the one built
With the money of Pedro
Ansurez and his wife.

Outside our Parish Church
Stood a young Adonis,
Who'd clearly wooed many
An unsuspecting Venus

And provoked jealousy
In a thousand angry Mars.

My heart gave a violent thump:
Love came like a policeman
Beating harshly on my door.

He caught my eyes, I tripped
And fell and then I fell
Again, this time from grace:
A sinful smile lit up
My face; a satin shoe
Lay upon the pavement.

Removing a glove to take
My hand in his (how like cold
Marble was that caress!) he
Lightly addressed me: "Lady,
Let me help you up; an
Angel should not fall so low".

I gave him a white lace
Glove to signify my
Thanks, and with that small
Token gave away my soul.

All afternoon I drank
Deeply from the dangerous
Potion of his handsome
Looks and lordly easy ways.

At our parting he spoke
Many lies; he spoke of
Love, trust, devotion,
And almost cried as we
Murmured our first goodbyes.

I wandered home in bliss;
You'll know my state of mind
If you've ever been in love;
I couldn't rest or find peace;
Sleep was just impossible.

At dawn I stumbled out of
Bed on to the balcony
And with red eyes looked down
On yesterday's Adonis.

That was the first ambush
In his campaign of love,
His war against my honour.

Every day he'd send me
Letters full of passion
And every night he would
Fill my ears with love songs.

When I accepted his gifts
Of diamond rings I felt
A debt of gratitude;
And there was only one
Thing I could give to him.

Oh, Quintana, why do
I burden you with this?

It took eight weeks for
Martin de Guzman, the name
Of my unfaithful love, to
Consummate his victory.

The master stroke of his
Cunning plan was an oath:
He swore he'd marry me
And I was as quick to
Believe his treacherous
Words as his promise has
Been slow in coming true.

News of our amour reached
His father's ears (curse my luck
That he found out); he knew
Of my nobility but
Also of my poverty;
I was not rich enough to
Be his daughter-in-law.

A more profitable
Marriage was sought, and one
Dona Ines discovered.
She lives locally and
Is blessed with a dowry
Of seventy thousand ducats.

He couldn't pursue the deal

Openly in case knowledge
Of my dishonour emerged
To jeopardize this most
Lucrative arrangement.

Listen to his solution:
The old man sent his son
Off quickly to Madrid,
The home of all deceit,
With the instruction to
Present himself under
The false name of Don Gil.

A letter was written
To Don Pedro Mendoza,
The father of my rival,
Dona Ines, expressing
Heartfelt sorrow that his
Headstrong son had got himself
Betrothed to a noble
But poor young woman called
Dona Juana Solis, who
Though an attractive girl,
Was not quite the match he'd
Expected for his son, with
A little note about the
Dangers of noblewomen
With beauty but without
Dowries in these hard times.
He begged Don Pedro to
Accept his apologies
And a substitute groom
For the dear Ines: a man
By the name of Don Gil.

But suspicion, the lynx-eyed
Vigilant of the soul, sensed
I was to be betrayed.

I sold two diamond rings
And with the gold I bought
Some closely guarded secrets.

I uncovered the entire
Scheme and saw clearly the

Aching distance between
What a man will promise
And what a man will do.

Exchanging a maiden's
Fear for womanly strength,
And armed with a richer
Sense of worldly wisdom,
I assumed this disguise:
Setting off to right the wrongs
Which greed has planned for me.

Don Martin has been in
Madrid for two days at most,
And my heart can guess his
Every move: he'll have dressed
Himself up in some new
Fancy clothes and with his
Mouth full of politeness
And deceit he'll go straight
To the house of Don Pedro
Mendoza and Ines.

Since I must be the spike to
Puncture this dishonesty,
I must keep Don Martin
Constantly in my sight,
Reducing his schemes to dust.

How will I achieve this?
I'm not sure yet but leave
That to me; he will not
Recognise me dressed like this,
But you, Quintana,
Must not be seen or you
May give away my plans.

Half a mile along that road
Lies Vallecas; go there
And I will write to you
With the news of all my
Victories and defeats.
We'll correspond via
The villagers who come

Daily from Vallecas
To sell their loaves of bread.

QUINTANA: Your story is worthy
Of the fables of Merlin.
Dona Juana, I don't know
What to say and I can't
Offer you advice; but
Whatever you dream of
Doing here in Madrid,
Please God you may achieve
All your aspirations.

DONA JUANA: Goodbye dear friend.

QUINTANA: You'll write?

DONA JUANA: Soon.

SCENE TWO

Dona Juana (dressed as a man) and Caramanchel.

CARA-
MANCHEL: If you want me to pay
My bill, Landlord, I'll be
Waiting on the bridge outside.

DONA JUANA: Hello!

CARA-
MANCHEL: Hello!

DONA JUANA: Have you run
Short of the price of a meal?

CARA-
MANCHEL: Say more.

DONA JUANA: I was just
Enquiring if you were
Looking for a master?

CARA-
MANCHEL: Yes, but if the heavens
Were to rain down masters,

Or if every insect
Changed into a master,
Or if masters went around
Crying out for lackeys,
Or the streets of Madrid
Were all paved with masters,
I still wouldn't find one;
I'm unlucky, you see,
When it comes to masters.

DONA JUANA: Have you suffered many?

CARA-
MANCHEL: Loads, and every one of them
A nightmare: I served
A doctor once, big beard,
Thick lips, but he wasn't
German; smart suits, velvet shoes,
Lemon silk accessories,
Lots of books but no cures.

After his surgery
He would always reserve
A medicinal draft
For himself: olives, stews,
Sides of ham and chicory;
He was never tempted to
Stuff himself with knowledge:
All the patients got were
Leeches and stale pots of pee.

He had a curious way
Of making diagnoses:
"Your malady, my lady,
Is a touch of wind and
Hypochondria", and then
He'd unbutton her dress
To feel congestion on her chest.

I never suffered the curse
Of a heavy pocket
In his employment, for
In matters of wages
His conscience weighed upon
Him extremely lightly.

DONA JUANA: He didn't pay you fairly?

CARA-
MANCHEL: It would be fair to say
When it came to money
His memory was as good
As his skill in curing
Anyone of anything.

After that I worked for
A narcissistic barrister
Who'd only take on cases
Which could earn him easy cash.

It made me so angry to
See his waiting room full
Of poor anxious plaintiffs
While he lounged in his office
Combing his greasy hair
And waxing his moustache.

DONA JUANA: A lackey with scruples?

CARA-
MANCHEL: Why not? Next I waited
On a pot-bellied priest
Who wouldn't say a word
To save a starving sinner
But was very eloquent
When thinking of his dinner.

"Ah how good is the Lord",
He'd sigh with eyes to heaven
And hands on well fed stomach,
Now tell me, Caramanchel,
What Holy man only called
God good when he had dined.

He expected his staff
To observe every fast day
While he made himself fat.
It was blind hypocrisy!
I bawled him out; that was that.

Six lean months I skivvied
For a penniless knight
Who spent his time dreaming

Of a worthy cause to fight.
Most weeks it dawned on him
A lackey needed payment
But when money got tight
He forgot our arrangement.

I thought it quite unfair
That I had to go hungry;
I'm not sure if he noticed
Or simply didn't care.
He had a novel way
Of saying the Lord's Prayer:
"Give me this day your daily
Bread", and of course Caramanchel did.

So sadly I was forced
Into embezzlement:
His poor horse subsisted
On half a peck of straw a week
Which I peddled on the side;
So I saw off starvation
But the horse nearly died.
I couldn't live like that.

Then I went to work for
A certain Lord Elderly
Who'd married a very, young lady
Near the end of his life;
The peculiarity
Of our contract was that
He expected me to serve him
While servicing his wife.

If I was to tell you
About all the bizarre
Masters I've ever had,
And I've had more than there
Are blisters on a leper,
You'd be asleep before
I got half way down the list.
No, I am unemployed
Because I am honest.

DONA JUANA: If you collect masters
Who are a little strange,

                    Then add me to your list.
                    I'm offering you a job.

CARA-
MANCHEL: Is this some sort of joke?
                    Whoever saw a page
                    Who had his own lackey?

DONA JUANA: I'm not a page; I'll have
                    You know I enjoy a private
                    Income; in fact I've come
                    To Madrid to enforce
                    A legal claim; my servant
                    Is not in good health and
                    Has had to remain in
                    Segovia.

CARA-
MANCHEL: You've come
                    To Madrid for justice?
                    Young man, you'll go home old.

DONA JUANA: I like your sense of humour.

CARA-
MANCHEL: I've never had a poet or
                    A eunuch for a master;
                    You, Sir, remind me of both.
                    As for payment I won't
                    Stipulate any fee;
                    Pay me what you think I'm worth;
                    I'm loyal and hardworking.

DONA JUANA: What's your name?

CARA-
MANCHEL: Caramanchel,
                    After the place where I
                    Was born.

DONA JUANA: I like your cheek
                    And your clever way with words.

CARA-
MANCHEL: What's your name?

DONA JUANA: Don Gil.

CARA-
MANCHEL: Don Gil
                Of what?

DONA JUANA: Don Gil, that's all.

CARA-
MANCHEL: So you've got no surname,
             And if one takes a closer
             Look at your chin you don't
             Seem to have a beard either.

DONA JUANA: It's important I conceal
             My surname for the present.
             Do you know of an inn
             That's respectable and clean?

CARA-
MANCHEL: I'll find us something cheap and
             Cheerful.

DONA JUANA: With a landlady?

CARA-
MANCHEL: And what a woman!

DONA JUANA: Really?

CARA-
MANCHEL: Really good!

DONA JUANA: On what street?

CARA-
MANCHEL: Urasos Street.

DONA JUANA: Let's go.
             (Aside) Tomorrow I shall trace
             The house of Don Pedro.
             Madrid, open your arms
             And embrace a stranger
             Who is new to town.

CARA-
MANCHEL: (Aside) What a beautiful unbroken
             Little voice he's got.

DONA JUANA: Are you coming, Caramanchel?

CARA-
MANCHEL: Don Gil, young Sir, let's go!

SCENE THREE

The house of Don Pedro.

Enter Don Pedro, Don Martin, Osorio.

DON PEDRO: *(Reading a letter.)* And finally, dear friend,
                    I must lament the youthful
                    Folly of my headstrong son;
                    For Don Martin has got
                    Himself betrothed to a
                    Noble but poor young woman,
                    One Dona Juana Solis,
                    Who though an attractive
                    Girl is not the kind of match
                    I had planned for my son.

                    I need not tell you of
                    The dangers which penniless
                    Noblewomen present to
                    We fathers in these hard times.
                    What had to happen happened:
                    He of course regretted it,
                    And she of course pressed her claim.

                    You can imagine how I feel
                    In being forced to forfeit
                    Your considerate offer;
                    A marriage between our
                    Two children would have changed
                    Our ancient friendship into
                    A blood relationship.
                    Please accept my regrets and
                    Convey my apologies
                    And kind greetings to your
                    Dear daughter, Dona Ines.

                    Although Fortune has frowned
                    On me, I feel she now turns
                    To smile upon you in this:

Don Gil de Albornoz,
The man who bears this letter,
Is a most eligible
And respectable man and
I've offered the match to him.

His wisdom, blood and prospects
(He is soon to inherit
Ten thousand ducats a year)
Should allow you to forget
My failure in this respect;
And shall leave me envious
Of your immense good fortune.
Any honour you may pay
To Don Gil will, I feel,
Be paid to me; Don Martin
Expresses his sorrow
And begs leave to kiss your hand.

Send me all the good news
Of your health and family
Which may heaven increase
Etc. etc. Valladolid,
July etc.
Don Andreas de Guzman.

DON PEDRO: *(To Don Martin.)* Don Gil, let me welcome
You a thousand times into
This house, your second home.
Your person is ample proof
Of the praise lavished on you
In this letter from my friend.

Fine prospects faced my daughter
And it would have warmed my heart
To bind my house in blood
To that of Don Andreas.
We have been friends since
We were boys, a bond which has
Developed into deep love;
Such relationships are not
Easily forgotten.

Unfortunately we have
Not met for many years;

I had hoped to occupy
My retirement in joining
Our estates, as we have
Joined our hearts, by sharing
What we hold most dearly.

However, as Don Martin
Has slipped, as young men will,
And nullified the contract,
I'm so glad you have been sent
To rectify the matter.

I will not say Ines
Has found a better husband,
That would insult my friend,
But though it remains unsaid,
Be sure I think it true.

DON MARTIN: Don Pedro, how can I
Compete with you when you
Do me so much honour?
What words could I speak to
Properly repay you?
The victory is yours and
I can only indicate
My gratitude by silence.

I will not tire you by
Declaring that your life
Is now dearer to me than
My own or any of those
Well worn compliments.

I have relatives at court,
Some of them titled, who can
Confirm the claims made on my
Behalf by Don Andreas.

However I am anxious
To be married quickly,
And alas, you must know as
Well as I the ways of court.

Any delay will further
My father in his designs:
He wishes to marry me to

A girl from Valladolid
Who is not of my choosing.
If he learned of my desire
To marry against his will
He would be so enraged that,
Should he survive the shock,
He would make all effort to
Sabotage the joy which you
Can offer me in secret.

DON PEDRO: The signature of my friend
Is enough to remove the
Need to seek any other
Confirmation of your worth.
Don Gil, you and I have come
To a firm agreement;
I would give Ines to you
If you were the poorest
Of gentlemen, as long
As Don Andreas chose
To champion your claim.

DON MARTIN: *(Aside to Osorio.)* Osorio, I think he's
Fallen for it.

OSORIO: *(Aside to Don Martin.)* Commit
Him to a date before
Dona Juana arrives
To upset all your plans.

DON MARTIN: *(Aside to Osorio.)* Everything is going well.

DON PEDRO: Don Gil, I think it might
Be a little imprudent to
Overwhelm Ines with this
Unexpected pleasure.
This afternoon she is due
To attend a gathering
At the Garden of the Duke,
Where you may introduce
Yourself informally
To her and suggest something
Of your intentions.

DON MARTIN: Oh Ines,
My dearest one! May the sun

                    Arrest its course that the day
                    On which I first witness your
                    Beauty may last forever.

DON PEDRO: If you have not yet prepared
                    A lodging place and my own
                    Home merits your approval,
                    I would be honoured to
                    Accept you as my guest.

DON MARTIN: Naturally I would be
                    Delighted to stay in
                    This house, soon to be the home
                    Of all my happiness;
                    However arrangements
                    Have already been made for
                    Me to stay nearby in a
                    Residence belonging to
                    My cousin.

DON PEDRÓ: I'll meet you at
                    The garden.

DON MARTIN: God protect you.

<u>SCENE FOUR</u>

Dona Ines and Don Juan.

DONA INES: If you keep up with this
                    Jealous harping I will
                    Never finish dressing.

DON JUAN: You're very keen to finish.

DONA INES: You're so sad today, and odd.

DON JUAN: Shouldn't a tortuous
                    Situation make one sad?
                    If you value my life,
                    Please don't go to the Garden.

DONA INES: But I have to go; Cousin
                    Clara has invited me.

DON JUAN: How easily a feigned

Excuse rolls off the tongue
When desire begins to fade.

DONA INES: Why should you fret if I've been
Invited to a party
At the Garden of the Duke?

DON JUAN: A sense of forboding
Promises some painful
Happening and even my
Love cannot assuage the fear
In my soul; Dona Ines,
Do you really have to go?

DONA INES: Just come with me and you'll
See that it's only
In your sick fantasies
That I'm unfaithful

DON JUAN: You're the queen of my heart.
How can I disobey you?

DONA INES: Constant jealousy creates
The event that it so fears;
But be assured, Don Juan,
I want you for my husband.
I'll see you this afternoon
At the Duke's lovely Garden.

DON PEDRO: *(Aside)* She's promised him her hand!

DON JUAN: I'll be there, full of fear.
Goodbye.

DONA INES: God keep you well.

Exit Don Juan.

SCENE FIVE

Don Pedro and Dona Ines.

DON PEDRO: Ines!

DONA INES: Sir, you must
Have come to tell me not

To forget my new cloak;
I expect you know my
Cousin's waiting for me.

DON PEDRO: I'm shocked by your promise
Of marriage to Don Juan.
Have I been so slow in
Finding you a husband?
Are you so old and wrinkled
That you'd risk sending me
To an early grave with your
Undercover promises?
What was Don Juan doing here?

DONA INES: Don't be cross; it isn't fair!
I promised him my hand
Assuming your approval;
And would you not profit
By him as a son-in-law?
Do you know how much he's worth?

DON PEDRO: You'll have a better husband,
So pull in the reins of
Your improper desire.
I didn't want to reveal
My intentions quite so soon
But your haste leaves me no choice.
I haven't yet decided
Who you're to marry but
You must stop this wanton
Behaviour straight away.

A wealthy young nobleman
Of excellent prospects
Has recently come to
Town from Valladolid.
You can meet him before
We proceed any further.

He's worth ten thousand ducats
A year in rents alone
And he'll inherit more.

As for your promise to
Don Juan, I'll sort that out.

DONA INES: There are lots of eligible
Men about who come from Madrid.
Why shackle me to a yokel?

Madrid is an ocean, is it not?
And Valladolid is a stream.
Why ignore the treasures of the sea
For the bounty of a brook?

And do you think it just to
Marry me to some unknown man
When I'm perfectly in love?

If it's simply your love
Of money which drives you
To this, then see it for
What it is: a sin which
Disfigures many fathers.

What's his name?

DON PEDRO: Don Gil.

DONA INES: Don Gil!
A spouse from a puppet show?
Gil! What a horrid name!
Does he have a shepherd's crook
And wear a sheepskin coat?

DON PEDRO: Why should you worry about
The name if the owner
Is noble and wealthy?
Just take a look at him
This afternoon and I'm
Sure you will fall in love.

DONA INES: I'm sure! Clara is still
Waiting in the coach outside.
(Aside) I'm not looking forward
To this trip at all now.

Give me my cloak.

DON PEDRO: He'll be there.
I've sent him to meet you.

DONA INES: (Aside) Me married to a Gil?
Do I look like a bumpkin?

SCENE SIX

In the garden of the Duke.

Dona Juana.

DONA JUANA: I have managed to acquire
Some vital information:
Don Pedro is due to
Arrive at this garden
Party with his daughter,
Dona Ines, whom he
Intends to introduce
To my faithless Don Martin.

Fortune, you have helped
Me find out where she lives
And whom she loves and all
Her father's marriage schemes;
These I will frustrate if
You remember my sorrow;
Please don't let me down.

I have gained the trust of
A servant in my rival's
House who is privy to
Her every conversation.
Miracles can be worked with
A small renumeration.

SCENE SEVEN

Dona Juana and Caramanchel.

CARA-
MANCHEL: *(Unaware of Dona Juana.)* My mysterious new
Master, the hermaphrodite
Don Gil, swore he'd meet me here.

I'm beginning to think
He's a ghost in disguise
Who has come to Madrid to
Rid me of my sanity.

> If I find proof of my
> Suspicion, I'll report
> Him to an officer of
> The Holy Inquisition.

DONA JUANA: Caramanchel.

CARA-
MANCHEL: Master!
> What wind blows you to this park.

DONA JUANA: A lady who reminds
> Me of a summer breeze.
> I'm thirsty for her beauty.

CARA-
MANCHEL: Her beauty makes you thirsty?
> That's an awful addiction;
> It's cheaper than whisky
> But it won't make you drunk.
> Is it love?

DONA JUANA: I adore her.

CARA-
MANCHEL: You shouldn't pose any
> Problem whatsoever
> In the game of love: if
> Your beard is anything
> To go by, you won't get
> Anyone into trouble.
> *(Music offstage.)*
> What's that music?

DONA JUANA: It heralds
> The entrance of my lady
> Who has flown down from heaven
> To adorn this garden.
> Stay in hiding and watch my
> Performance.

CARA-
MANCHEL: Well what's he like
> My master, a capon
> Who wants to play the cock?

SCENE EIGHT

Don Juan, Dona Ines and Dona Clara in fancy dress, Dona Juana and Caramanchel.

SONG: Trees of the field,
Fountains of the Duke,
Wake up my young mistress
For she must hear my song.

Ask her to compare
Her beauty and cruelty
With the depth of your streams
And my love and my pain.

Let your silver streams
Ripple, splash and fall to
Wake up my fair maiden
For she must hear my song.

DONA CLARA: What a beautiful garden!

DONA INES: This vine, which wraps itself
About these poplar trees,
Creates a green canopy
Adorned as it were with
Emerald grapes, and forms
A natural shade for us
From the rigours of the sun.

DON JUAN: We are surrounded by
The fruit of Bacchus and
If he be the god of love
Perhaps these green grapes will
Console my lovesick heart.

DONA INES: Dona Clara, sit by me;
Let us view this fountain:
Its clear crystal waters
Promise chaste, refreshing
Kisses to the thirsty.

DON JUAN: So the party has begun.
Is it vital that we came?

DONA INES: Yes my Lord, if only

                    To prove to you that my
                    Devotion is complete.

DONA JUANA: *(Aside)* Is she not beautiful?

CARA-
MANCHEL: *(Aside)* Well she's more beautiful
                    Than money but I fall
                    For money every time.

DONA JUANA: *(Aside)* I want to talk with her.

CARA-
MANCHEL: Now's your chance; talk away!

DONA JUANA: Fair Lady, I kiss your hand,
                    And beg your permission to
                    Join your company at this
                    Masquerade; I am but
                    A stranger to Madrid.

DONA CLARA: We would be insulted
                    If you didn't join us!

DONA INES: Where does your most noble
                    Lordship come from?

DONA JUANA: I was
                    Born in Valladolid.

DONA INES: Don Juan, move along and
                    Make room for this young man.

DON JUAN: *(Aside)* I suppose I must yield
                    My seat with courtesy;
                    My heart aches with jealousy.

DONA INES: *(Aside)* What a dramatic presence
                    And what a gorgeous face.

DON JUAN: *(Aside)* Is she making eyes at him?
                    Yes, I must control my rage.

DONA INES: So your Lordship comes from
                    Valladolid? Do you know
                    Don Gil by any chance,
                    A gentleman of your town
                    Who has just come to Madrid?

DONA JUANA: Don Gil of what?

DONA INES: Who knows what?
            Can there be more than one
            Don Gil in all the world?

DONA JUANA: Does the name repel you?

DONA INES: Who'd believe that anyone
            Would attach the title
            Don to Gil: Gil the shepherd
            In a smock who's sung about
            In horrid little folk songs.

CARA-
MANCHEL: Gil is worthy of respect!
            Gil pays my wages!

DONA JUANA: Silence!

CARA-
MANCHEL: My Master's called Don Gil.
            It's a perfectly good name.
            There's parochial, bronchial.

DONA JUANA: I myself am Don Gil,
            At your service, My Lady.

DONA INES: You're Don Gil.

DONA JUANA: Indeed I'm he;
            But should my name displease you
            I'll be baptised again.
            I am no longer Gil
            But who you'd have me be.

DON JUAN: No one here gives a fig if
            You're called Gil or Catherine Gil.
            Please be polite and remain
            In the bounds of courtesy.

DONA JUANA: Forgive me, Sir, if I give
            Offence; I meant only
            To satisfy the lady.

DONA INES: I wish you'd calm down, Don Juan.

DON JUAN: What does it matter to us
            If he's called Gil or not?

DONA INES: *(Aside)* This must be the man who

      Has come to be my husband.
      I'm so taken with his looks;
      He's awfully handsome.

DONA JUANA: I apologise if I've
      Given you displeasure, Sir.

DON JUAN: And you must pardon me, Sir.
      I have overstepped the mark;
      My temper's abated now.

DONA CLARA: Let the harmony of
      The music bring you peace.

      They stand.

DONA INES: *(To Don Juan.)* Your Lordship, shall we dance?

DON JUAN: *(Aside)* So Don Gil is my rival;
      Well, let fate do what it will
      For Ines will be mine;
      And if he competes with me
      And flirts with her, he will
      Discover that he's playing
      A very dangerous game.

DONA INES: Will you come?

DON JUAN: I won't dance.

DONA INES: Will you, Don Gil?

DONA JUANA: I don't want
      To cause this man distress.

DON JUAN: My anger's gone; please dance.

DONA INES: Yes, you can dance with me.

DON JUAN: *(Aside)* My obligation to
      Courtesy costs me dearly.

DONA CLARA: *(Aside)* This young Don Gil is an
      Angel cut from crystal.
      I'll be the shadow of
      This gentle, graceful man.

      Dona Ines, I'd like
      To take this dance with you.

DONA INES: *(Aside)* Don Gil is a precious jewel.
           I'm dying for his embrace.

               The three ladies dance.

SONG: To the water mill of love
           Ran the happy young maiden
           And slowly the mill wheel
           Ground all her hope to flour.
           May Mary bring her peace.

           Love makes its daily bread
           From young grains of joyousness.
           Harsh stones of jealousy
           Crush the grains into flour.

           As she sat by the bankside,
           Sweet dreams of her lover
           Flowed as freely as water,
           And she sang to the river:

           "You ripples of the water,
           When you see my lover,
           Dance on the pebbles,
           Sing him a lullaby.

           You birds in your nests,
           When you see my lover,
           Fly down from the trees
           And crown him with blossom."

           The oxen of suspicion
           Came and drank at the river;
           When they are present
           Hope is soon drained away.

           And when the young maiden
           Saw the water mill of love
           Had come to a standstill,
           She asked it a question:

           "Dear Mill of Love, dear Mill,
           Why is your water wheel still?
           Dear Mill of Love, dear Mill,
           Why is your water wheel still?"

           "The oxen of suspicion
           Have drunk all my water.

> The oxen of suspicion
> Have drunk all my water."

> Then she met Love Herself
> All covered in white flour
> From grinding down the souls
> Of unhappy lovers.

> And she sang out to Love,
> "You are a grinding stone,
> Love, you are a miller,
> Love, you are a miller."

> And Love said, "If you're afraid,
> You had better run away,
> For when you're in love,
> I will grind you into flour."

They finish dancing.

DONA INES : *(Aside to Dona Juana.)* Don Gil of a thousand charms,
At every step of the dance
My heart exploded with love.
I know that you have come to
Madrid to be my husband.
Forgive the ungrateful soul
That I am if I refused,
Before I'd even met you,
To accept the joy that I
Now impatiently await.
I'm utterly in love
With you.

DONA CLARA :   *(Aside)* I'm utterly
In love with this Don Gil.
He's such a little pearl.

DONA JUANA : *(Aside to Dona Ines.)* Words alone are not enough
To pay the debt I owe you.
Your escort is staring
At me suspiciously;
Dona Ines, I must leave you.

DONA INES : Are you jealous?

DONA JUANA :   Not at all.

DONA INES : Do you know where I live?

DONA JUANA: Yes.

DONA INES: Will you come to grace my house?
            Soon you will be its lord.

DONA JUANA: I will come to you tonight.

DONA INES: Then I will keep constant
            Watch from my window.

DONA JUANA: Goodbye.

DONA INES: *(Aside)* Oh no, dear me, he's going!
            Promise you'll come!

DONA JUANA: I promise.

Exit Dona Juana and Caramanchel.

SCENE NINE

Dona Ines, Dona Clara, Don Juan.

DONA INES: Don Juan, you're always moody.

DON JUAN: Melancholy is my friend
            For it helps me see the truth
            Of your wanton fickle heart.
            Clearly my suspicions were
            Not ill founded, Dona Ines.

DONA INES: My father is coming;
            Please stop being unhappy;
            Save it until later.

DON JUAN: You monster! I'm going.
            Ines, you'll pay for this.

Exit Don Juan.

DONA INES: He's so obsessive, Clara,
            But Don Gil's foot means more
            To me than a prince's hand.

SCENE TEN

Don Pedro, Don Martin, Dona Ines, Dona Clara.

DON PEDRO: Ines.

DONA INES: Oh my dearest
                 Father, Don Gil is not a man;
                 He's the spirit of grace,
                 The essence of wit and
                 The source of joyousness
                 Guarded by love in the
                 Secret vaults of heaven.

                 As soon as I saw him,
                 I fell; I adore him;
                 My soul is aching at the
                 Prospect of the wasted
                 Days between now and the
                 Fulfilment of my longing.

DON PEDRO: *(Aside to Don Martin.)* Don Gil, when did she see you?

DON MARTIN: I've no idea, unless
                 It was on my journey from
                 My lodging to this Garden.

DON PEDRO: That's time enough, Don Gil,
                 You've worked a miracle;
                 It must be your charisma;
                 Go up to her and thank her.

DON MARTIN: Dona Ines, I don't
                 Know who I should praise for
                 The good fortune that seems
                 To bless my every step.

                 Is it possible that
                 Having had the merest
                 Glimpse of me, you have
                 Come to this happy state?
                 Is it possible that
                 You embrace my proposal
                 So soon?

DONA INES: What? Who? You must
                 Be completely insane.
                 Do you think that I'm in
                 Love with you? I've never
                 Even seen you. Is this
                 Another of your tricks?

DON PEDRO: My child, are you quite well?

DON MARTIN: *(Aside)* My God, what's happening?

DON PEDRO: You said you'd seen Don Gil.

DONA INES: And so I have.

DON PEDRO: You said
You liked his looks.

DONA INES: Oh yes!
He's an angel!

DON PEDRO: You said
You'd be his wife.

DONA INES: What's this?
You're making me upset.

DON MARTIN: I say Don Gil is here.

DONA INES: What?

DON PEDRO: Don Gil, the man you praised!

DON MARTIN: Dear Ines, I am Don Gil.

DONA INES: You! Don Gil!

DON MARTIN: Yes.

DONA INES: Nonsense!

DON PEDRO: Ines, I swear he is.

DONA INES: Don Gil with a hairy face?
The Gil whom I adore is
A beardless boy, a gentle
Gil in emerald green.

DON PEDRO: She is quite clearly mad.

DON MARTIN: Dona Ines, I am
Don Gil from Valladolid.

DONA INES: That's where my Don Gil is from.

DON PEDRO: Ines, mad child, you're wrong.

DON MARTIN: In Valladolid there is
No one called Don Gil, but me.

DON PEDRO: What does this man look like?
            Now please try and concentrate.

DONA INES: His face is shining gold;
            His words are sweetest honey;
            And his breeches are a
            Beautiful shade of green;
            Oh they aren't really breeches
            But a gift from heaven.

DON PEDRO: Don Gil! Don Gil of what?

DONA INES: Don Gil of the green breeches,
            That is what I'll call him.
            That's enough.

DON PEDRO: She seems to have
            Taken complete leave of her
            Senses, and Dona Clara,
            What's the matter with you?

DONA CLARA: Don Gil will be my husband.

DONA INES: You!

DONA CLARA: Yes, me; I'm going home
            To tell my mother; she'll help
            To make me Don Gil's wife.

DONA INES: I'll rip your heart out first.

DON MARTIN: Who is this new Don Gil?

DON PEDRO: Your madness will force me . . .

DONA INES: I've agreed to wed Don Gil
            So why are you so angry?

DON MARTIN: Ines, I am Don Gil.
            Let me fulfil your dreams.

DONA INES: Don Gil of the green breeches,
            He's my man.

DON PEDRO: She seems to
            Have fallen in love with
            A pair of green breeches.
            Whoever heard such a thing?

DON MARTIN: Green breeches! I'll get a pair
                     If that will do the trick.

DON PEDRO: Go home you lunatic.

DONA INES: Oh my Don Gil, my soul.

END OF ACT ONE

ACT TWO

SCENE ONE

A room in Juana's newly rented accommodation.

Dona Juana (as a woman) and Quintana.

QUINTANA: You are without equal!
I can't believe my ears
Or imagine the sequel
To this masquerade of yours.
However I never
Knew a woman run short
Of imagination.

DONA JUANA: Quintana, let me tell you
The present situation:

Dona Ines has fallen
Head over heals in love
With me and is quite absorbed
In her infatuation.

Don Martin is out hunting
The mysterious Don Gil
Who seems to have stolen
Both his name and his bride.

As I'm doing my utmost
To avoid him while I'm out,
He is utterly bemused;
He believes he's haunted
By some vindictive sprite.

Don Pedro has lost all
Patience with his daughter who
Cares nothing for his wishes
And still less for Don Martin.

She swears she will be the wife
Of no one but Don Gil and
Interrogates each caller
To the house without mercy;
If I don't show up soon she

                    Will violate her honour:
                    She's even been threatening
                    To take away her life.

QUINTANA: Now you're a missing person
                    She'll send out a search party.

DONA JUANA: Her servants have already
                    Been assigned to that duty.
                    When they ask her to describe
                    My distinguishing features
                    She tells them to look out
                    For my nice green breeches.
                    There is a certain Don Juan,
                    A man she used to want to wed,
                    Who is so madly jealous
                    That he wants to see me dead.

QUINTANA: Mistress, please be careful
                    How you play this game,
                    Your very soul is at stake;
                    Consider the fires of hell.

DONA JUANA: I've yet to make a mistake;
                    Dona Clara loves me
                    As well! She's the cousin
                    Of my rival and she's
                    Also suicidal.

                    Her over anxious mother
                    Has promised to match Clara
                    To the elusive Don Gil.

QUINTANA: You will make quite a catch.

DONA JUANA: This widow is wasting
                    Her money on messengers
                    Who are scouring Madrid
                    With a continuous chorus:

                    "Have you seen a man in green
                    Called Don Gil of Valladolid?"

QUINTANA: You will soon be infamous.

DONA JUANA: Quintana, after we
                    Parted company on
                    Segovia Bridge, I

Met and hired a lackey.
He's extremely annoyed
As he's hardly seen me
Since the day he was employed.
I can't help laughing when
I look out of my window
And see him searching for
Me up and down the street.

I overheard him discuss
My absence with Ines:
Her theory is that a witch
Has made me disappear;
He says I'm more likely
To be laid out in a ditch,
A victim of the venom
Of the jilted Don Juan.

QUINTANA: Is there a chance your lackey
              Will call in the law?

DONA JUANA: Possibly,
              He's besotted with me,
              And very brave and loyal.

QUINTANA: What's his name?

DONA JUANA: Caramanchel.

QUINTANA: And why have you chosen now
              To change into your frock?

DONA JUANA: New ploys and plots and schemes to
            Block the plans of Don Martin.
            Yesterday I rented this
            Fully furnished house with
            A servant in residence.

QUINTANA: Why all this extravagance?

DONA JUANA: To get close to Ines
            Whom Don Martin wants to wed!
            She lives immediately next door:
            There's just a wall between us.

            I contrived a meeting
            This morning, and while we
            Paid the compliments due

> To new neighbours we soon
> Became the best of friends.
> Apparently I look
> Exactly like the man
> She loves in green breeches.
>
> It seems my presence teaches
> Her some solace in his
> Inexplicable absence.
>
> Now we are on such terms
> Of intimacy I can
> Glean all the movements of
> Don Martin; and be on hand
> To sabotage his plans.

QUINTANA: You're the picture of deceit.

DONA JUANA: And I shall be my own cure.

QUINTANA: By taking the liberty
Of two homes in Madrid?

DONA JUANA: With a servant and a lackey.

QUINTANA: But what about the money?

DONA JUANA: I've some diamond rings to sell.

QUINTANA: And when you've run out of rings?

DONA JUANA: Then dear Dona Ines
Shall have to subsidise me;
A woman in love is soon
Parted from her money.

QUINTANA: Not in my experience.

I'm going back to
Vallecas; you have told
Enough lies to deserve
A litigation.

DONA JUANA: Not lies;
These are inspirations.

QUINTANA: They are sure to inspire
You to change your dress at
Least twenty times today.

DONA JUANA: I will change as often
As necessary to
Achieve my remedy.

Quintana, I have just
Had an idea of how you
Can help me before you go
Back to Vallecas.
I want you to pretend
You have just made a journey
Here from Valladolid.
Say that you are carrying
Some secret letters for
Don Martin.

QUINTANA: What trick is this?

DONA JUANA: The strangest fantasies
Assail my husband's mind:
He thinks I'm in Madrid;
He thinks it me who's trying
To spoil his wedding plans
And that young Don Gil is me!

To put his troubled mind
At rest, you must tell him
These letters were written
By me in Valladolid.

In them I'll simulate
All kinds of female complaints,
You know the usual nonsense,
And you can embellish
The tale as much as you like.
Why don't you say I'm pregnant
And locked up in a convent,
Screaming with the agony
Of unrequited love?

Warn him my father may
Yet hear of my condition
And could easily take leave
Of the little sense he's got.
You might wish to suggest
He has an evil temper
And is likely to avenge

Me with a brutal garrotte.

This should set Don Martin's
Mind completely at rest:
He will know for certain
I am not in Madrid
Dressed up in green breeches.

QUINTANA: I think I'd better go.

DONA JUANA: And I'd better get writing.

QUINTANA: You'll give me the letters?

DONA JUANA: Disappear quickly, I've got
            A guest.

QUINTANA: Who?

DONA JUANA: Dona Ines!

SCENE TWO

Dona Ines (with a cloak) and Don Juan.

DONA INES: If this is not about love,
             What's the point of jealousy?

DON JUAN: Not about love?

DONA INES: The secret
             Of nature's beauty is
             Said to reside in her
             Wonderful diversity.
             I'm being really perverse
             To increase my beauty.

DON JUAN: If nature is beautiful
             Because she is diverse,
             You must be the loveliest
             Woman in the world; you are
             Certainly the most perverse.
             Are you to shatter my heart
             For a beardless boy? You don't
             Even know his family name!
             Oh Dona Ines, will you
             Leave me for this upstart?

DONA INES: Please stop whining, Don Juan,
             Do I have to remind
             You we are not at home?

DON JUAN: You inconstant woman!
             You shall never caress
             The boyish face of this
             Don Gil; I'll kill him first!

DONA INES: But which Don Gil?

DON JUAN: How cruel!
             The importunate youth
             Who has stolen you from me.

DONA INES: Don Gil of the green breeches
             Is not the one who robs you
             Of your reason; I swear by
             God in heaven I've not
             Seen him since that afternoon.
             A second Don Gil is now
             On the scene.

DON JUAN: Are there two?

DONA INES: Yes!
             I suspect the young Don Gil
             Is operating under
             An assumed name to pull off
             Some kind of confidence trick.

             The Don Gil who tries to force
             You from my heart is the most
             Horrid Gil with a hairy face.
             My father insists I
             Marry the grizzly Gil
             And of course it is my
             Duty to obey him.
             But if you were to kill
             This new Don Gil (his surname
             Is De Albornoz) I'd be
             Eternally in your debt.

DON JUAN: You say that his name is
             Don Gil de Albornoz?

DONA INES: So I've been told; he's lodging

            In that nice house owned by
            The Count around the corner.

DON JUAN: So close?

DONA INES: To be near me!

DON JUAN: And you hate him?

DONA INES: Completely!

DON JUAN: If I can win your love
            By killing him then I
            Already feel the laurels
            Of victory on my brow.
            I'll make a solemn pledge:
            This new Don Gil will die.

SCENE THREE

Dona Ines.

DONA INES: If only it were done!
            This is the quickest way
            To open up the path
            To the young Don Gil who
            Owns my loving heart: for
            When his loathsome namesake's
            Dead I shall be free; then
            Father can cause me no
            Further pain with his most
            Selfish plan to marry me
            To a man I don't love
            At all; I cannot wait
            For my release; father's
            Greedy hopes will have to
            Remain unsatisfied.

SCENE FOUR

Dona Juana (as a woman), Dona Ines, Valdivieso.

DONA JUANA: Oh Dona Ines, you have come
              To see me in my house;
              What a privilege to
              Receive such a visitor.
              I was just going to
              Come and knock on your door.

              Can someone come and relieve
              Dona Ines of her cloak?

VALDIVIESO: *(Aside)* What are you talking about?
              How many housemaids do you
              Think you've hired? There's only one
              Servant in this house, that's me.

DONA JUANA: Oh dear, neither Vega nor
              Esperanza can be here
              As yet; it's such a trial
              Moving house: nothing and
              Nobody are where they
              Ought to be; Valdivieso,
              Would you kindly take this
              Cloak from Dona Ines?

              He does so and exits.

SCENE FIVE

Dona Juana and Ines.

DONA INES: Dona Elvira, I can't help
             Commenting on your graceful
             Style and enchanting features.

DONA JUANA: What honour you do me,
              Dona Ines, though I'm
              Sure you must be thinking
              About somebody else.
              Are you not drawn to me
              Because I look like the man
              Who is your heart's desire?

DONA INES: Oh no, Dona Elvira,
             Your beauty is uniquely

> Yours; though I won't deny your
> Remarkable resemblance
> To the man I adore,
> You deserve in your own right
> To be worshipped by some
> Adonis or Narcissus;
> Indeed the sun who shines
> Above should be enslaved
> By your exquisite eyes.

DONA JUANA: Once a man promised to
> Love me always; but then
> He deserted me.

DONA INES: Oh dear,
> I curse the man who could
> Cause you so much sorrow.
> What's his name?

DONA JUANA: Dona Ines,
> You have filled my eyes with tears;
> Please let's speak of matters
> Other than the memory
> Of my painful history.

DONA INES: Sharing your sorrow may bring
> Relief and you can trust me
> As your friend, Elvira,
> Tell me the sad story
> Of your heart; after all
> I've already told you mine.

DONA JUANA: I swear by your life it is
> Dull to listen to the woes
> Of another.

DONA INES: That's not true!

DONA JUANA: If you want to hear my tale
> You must prepare to weep:

> I came into the world
> In Burgos, capital of
> Old Castille; there my father,
> Rodrigo de Cisneros,
> Gave me life and all its pain.

Sadly I was born with
A vulnerable heart and
For as long as I can
Remember I have loved
Miguel de Ribera,
A man as handsome as he
Has been cruel to me.

In time he returned my love
But his passion was like small
Coins coming in large amounts
But disappearing quickly.

Our affair soon reached the point
Of no return: he opened
An account with me, his
Promises, my guarantee,
Oh yes, he swore we'd marry:
And a woman who believes
Words spoken in the heat
Of passion deserves all
She gets, or doesn't get.
Now do you see what happened?

He grew weary of me, ran
Away to Valladolid,
And since I am an orphan
I had no choice but to leave
Burgos in solitary
Pursuit of my lover.

When I confronted him
He excused his desertion
With sick lies; I need not
Explain to you how love
Riddled with dishonesty
Surely withers and dies.
Whilst in Valladolid,
Don Miguel stayed with a wise,
Wealthy and well born young man
Who was also his cousin:
One Don Gil de Albornoz.
This relation had a friend
Called Martin de Guzman.

What followed was that your
Father wrote to the father
Of Don Martin (his name is
Don Andreas) asking if
Don Martin might marry
The lovely Dona Ines,
Who hopefully is you?

However Don Martin
Had already promised
To be the husband of
A certain Dona Juana;
And because he would not break
His word to this woman,
He offered the prospective
Match to his friend, Don Gil, who
Hearing of your worthy
Person and estate could
Hardly wait to marry you.
He acquired some letters
Of introduction from
Don Andreas and set off
For Madrid to press his suit.

But before he left home he
Made the dreadful mistake of
Bragging about the beauty
And enormous dowry of
His intended to his friend,
My ungrateful husband,
The runaway Don Miguel: whose
Greedy imagination
Was set on fire; he fell in
Love with you simply by
Listening to Don Gil's
Description, at least of
Your dowry; for love is run
By bankers now and every
Heart contains a merchant.

Don Miguel ignored all
The obligations of
Friendship by stealing Don Gil's
Letters of introduction.

He arrived in Madrid
Less than a month ago
Masquerading under
The false name of Don Gil
In pursuit of your hand.
When Don Gil discovered this
Terrible deceit he gave
Chase to his erstwhile friend.
The two of us met by chance,
Exchanged our stories and
Decided to travel on
Together to Madrid.

I've been in this city nine
Long days and you are now the
Judge of my love; I await
The verdict you deliver.

One final twist: as we
Travelled along together
From Valladolid, the
Uncanny similarity
Between Don Gil and I
Fed a certain kind of
Intimacy; he saw
Himself in me and I in him.
He fell in love.

DONA INES :   With who?

DONA JUANA : With me.

DONA INES :   Don Gil de Albernoz?

DONA JUANA : Don Gil who is my mirror;
              It's as if an artist
              Had painted a pair of
              Perfect copies, yet each one
              A true original.

DONA INES : Does he wear green breeches?

DONA JUANA : As green as grass in Spring,
              As green as the man himself
              Who is an April day.

DONA INES : You praise him; do you love him?

DONA JUANA: I could love him very well;
After all, I'm a woman.

But my soul is forever
Attached to the cold heart
Of my inconstant husband.
Be strong, do not submit
Yourself to jealousy;
I spurned Don Gil at once.
And since my Don Miguel seemed
Close to fulfilling his
Wedding schemes, I rented
This house to observe closely
The climax of this awful tale
Of my humiliation.

DONA INES: So Don Miguel is a false
Don Gil who despite being
Your husband is trying
To have me as his wife?

DONA JUANA: Exactly!

DONA INES: So the true
Don Gil is the man who
Wears green breeches; oh dear,
Poor me, what can I do?

If my Don Gil is in
Love with you, that must be
Why he's disappeared; he's
Crying somewhere over you.

DONA JUANA: If you reject my Miguel,
I'll reject your Don Gil.

DONA INES: Elvira, it's a deal.
How can I marry a man
Who's already married?
Don't worry, I'll soon spurn him.

DONA JUANA: Come with me and watch while
I write Don Gil a letter
Which will kill any hopes
He nurtures in his heart
For me; then I'll ask my
Servant to deliver it.

DONA INES: Elvira, dearest, you are
             Awfully good to me;
             I'll always be your slave.

DONA JUANA: *(Aside)* She has stepped into my trap.
             Sometimes I am a woman
             And sometimes I am a man;
             Now Elvira and now Gil;
             For love I'll do anything.

                    Exit Dona Juana and Dona Ines.

SCENE SIX

A street near Don Martin's lodging.

Don Martin and Quintana.

DON MARTIN: What, Quintana, you've just left
             Your mistress in a convent?
             I find that hard to believe!

QUINTANA: It's true, Sir, I carried her
             To San Quirce myself;
             All the way she sighed and sobbed
             And moaned; I'm afraid to say
             Dona Juana is pregnant.

DON MARTIN: Pregnant?

QUINTANA: Nothing will stay
             In her stomach; she's retching
             Continuously; her skirt
             Is swelling like an egg,
             Her steps are slow and heavy
             And she's developed the
             Most curious cravings.

             Her father will never
             Forgive you if you don't
             Go to her assistance.
             What price her reputation
             If she gives birth to a
             Bastard in a convent?

DON MARTIN: Just let me tell you my
Theory about your mistress,
Quintana; I believe
She has run away from
Valladolid and is
Here in Madrid where she
Persecutes me daily.

QUINTANA: Sir! What a cruel and
Unjust thing to say about
The mother of your child.

DON MARTIN: I know she's capable
Of such wild behaviour.

QUINTANA: That poor innocent girl?
Why even at this moment
She will be on her knees
Beside her good sisters
Whispering penitential
Prayers for you; surely
These letters support my words.

DON MARTIN: Yes Quintana, I can't
Deny my responsibility
For the crimes she describes.
I came to Madrid with an
Urgent business problem
Which can only be resolved
By the King; Dona Juana
Would have found our parting
Difficult; I did not want
To delay my departure
By explaining why I
Had to go without her.

Now I know how badly
She has taken my attempt
To be diplomatic, and
That we are soon to be blessed
With a child, I shall make haste
To get home; I'll leave within
A week whether my business
Here is concluded or not.

QUINTANA: I'll be travelling home

          Tomorrow so I'll tell
          Dona Juana exactly what
          You've told me; and expect
          A fine reward for bringing
          Her such delightful news.

DON MARTIN: I'm sure you won't be
          Disappointed, and I must
          Give you some comforting
          Letters for the poor lady.
          Where are you residing?
          I can't take you to my
          Place for fear of spoiling
          A little plan of mine,
          Which I'll explain anon.

QUINTANA: I'm staying in a street near
          Meson de Parades.

DON MARTIN: Good.

QUINTANA: Why don't you give me the
          Letters in the morning
          On your way to the palace?
          I could meet you outside
          The main gate.

DON MARTIN: Marvellous!
          (Aside) I don't want him turning
          Up at my lodging asking
          For Don Martin de Guzman.
          That would ruin everything.

QUINTANA: *(Aside)* I think I'd better be off.

DON MARTIN: Until tomorrow, Quintana!

QUINTANA: *(Aside)* Where will all this lying end?

          Exit Quintana.

SCENE SEVEN

DON MARTIN: If I'm to be a father,
          That's enough, and if

Dona Juana is pregnant
With my baby, that's enough.

I've repaid the truth of her
Love with counterfeit money.

If I am soon to be blessed
With an heir in Valladolid,
What am I doing in Madrid
Trying to marry myself
Off to another woman?

These are not the actions
Of an honourable man.

The only way to redeem
This shameful situation
Is to shake off the dust
From this city and go home.

SCENE EIGHT

Don Martin and Don Juan.

DON JUAN: Don Gil de Albornoz,
Have you the courage in
Your heart to draw that sword
And risk your life? You are brave
Enough to force Ines
To wed you against her will.
I openly declare
A personal interest
In this affair and challenge
You to fight me on some field
Or bridge where we will not
Be seen by anyone;
Then we shall discover if
You're as valiant with a
Sword as you are in love.

DON MARTIN: Extinguish this fiery rage
Or my sword will pierce your
Clothes and snuff out your anger.
However, since I am

A reasonable man, I
Will not enter into
A duel without cause.

Let us take the case to
Dona Ines if you
Believe she abhors me.
Nature has given her
A tongue with which to answer
Yes or no; and if she gives
A yes to me and a no
To you, I will withdraw
My suit immediately.

DON JUAN: She's being forced by her
             Father to marry you;
             And I confess I love her
             And will not allow this
             Wrong to be done to her:
             So we must go and fight
             It out to the death unless
             You call off the wedding
             And surrender all your claims.

DON MARTIN: Has Dona Ines said she
             Will obey her father
             And be my wedded wife?

DON JUAN: She will obey her senile
             Father rather than her heart.

DON MARTIN: It would be very foolish
             Of me to risk all I have
             Achieved for the sake of
             Your jealousy; if Ines
             Has already answered yes
             To me, why should I take
             Up swords with you? I would
             Either kill you dead or
             Die myself and lose what
             I've clearly accomplished.
             Having won the right to
             Call Ines my wife, do you
             Really expect me to
             Jeopardize my life? No Sir,

Allow me to collect my prize.
We can always fight again.

DON JUAN :   You lack either courage or
              Respect; but the time will come
              When your suit proceeds less
              Favourably; then I shall
              Check your unwelcome love.

SCENE NINE

Don Martin.

DON MARTIN : If Ines is inclined
              To obey her father and
              Accept my suit, Juana,
              You must forgive me; and
              Love, if you would beckon
              Me homewards, it's time for
              You to change your direction.

              My increasing knowledge
              Of the beauty and value
              Of Dona Ines must
              Free me from any sense
              Of culpability.

SCENE TEN

Don Martin and Osorio.

OSORIO :   By the grace of God, I
              Have finally found you.

DON MARTIN : Osorio, how good
              To see you; any letters?

OSORIO :   Yes, Sir.

DON MARTIN :   From my father?

OSORIO :   On the post office wall
              Half way down the list by

The number seventeen,
There was indication
Of a parcel addressed
To a certain Don Martin.

DON MARTIN: It looks like an order
For immediate payment
Of some gold.

OSORIO: Let's hope so.

DON MARTIN: It's inscribed with the name of
Don Gil de Albornoz.

OSORIO: Your pseudonym; hurry up
And open it.

DON MARTIN: This says:
"To my dear son Don Martin"
And this says: "To Agustin
Solier de Carmargo,
City banker of Madrid."

OSORIO: Let Fortune kiss Agustin
If he can turn this paper
Into gold.

DON MARTIN: And that he can!

OSORIO: Just tell me where to go, Sir.

DON MARTIN: To Guadalajara Gate.

OSORIO: I wouldn't mind giving
This letter a kiss if
It's going to pay my wages;
We were nearly broke, Sir.

DON MARTIN: I'll read this personal
Letter to me before
You go, Osorio.

OSORIO: Fine.

DON MARTIN: *(Reads)* Dear Son, I am concerned to
Know the outcome of your
Petition, which according

> To your last letter began
> With such promise. In order
> To assist your efforts, I'm
> Enclosing a draft for one
> Thousand escudos as well as
> A letter for my banker
> In Madrid: Agustin Solier.
> The letter says the money's
> For Don Gil de Albornoz,
> A relative of mine,
> So don't collect it yourself
> (Agustin knows your face).
> Instead send Osorio
> In the character of
> Majordomo to Don Gil.
> Dona Juana Solis went
> Missing the day you left.
> Her household is seriously
> Worried and so am I.
> She is probably in
> Pursuit of you and may
> Try to prevent that which
> We all crave so dearly.
> Please bring everything
> To a speedy conclusion,
> And when you've settled
> A wedding date let me
> Know so I can set out
> At once and celebrate
> The end of these intrigues.
> May God bless you and keep you,
> Valladolid, August etc.
> Your father.

OSORIO: So Dona Juana is
                Missing from home?

DON MARTIN: I know
                Where she is; Quintana
                Has just given me this
                Letter from her; she's on
                A guided retreat in a
                A convent in San Quirce.
                Actually she's pregnant.

OSORIO: *(Aside)* Yet another tale of
                 An unmarried mother.

DON MARTIN: She left without a word
                 To her father; my silent
                 Exit left her in such
                 A state of jealous rage
                 That she didn't trust herself
                 To speak to anyone.
                 That will explain her household's
                 Confusion referred to
                 In my father's letter.
                 I'll write a reassuring
                 Letter to Dona Juana
                 And when I've married Ines
                 I'll write to her again with
                 The opinion that it would
                 Be best for all concerned if
                 She pursued her vocation.

OSORIO: If she's buried herself
                 In San Quirce she must
                 Already know her fate!

SCENE ELEVEN

Aguilar, Don Martin, Osorio.

AGUILAR: Can that be his Lordship,
                 Don Gil de Albornoz?

DON MARTIN: Aguilar, my old friend!

AGUILAR: Sir, I bring the best of news.
                 Don Pedro requests your
                 Immediate presence at
                 His house for he intends
                 To wed you to his daughter
                 Even if he has to dam
                 The river of her tears.

DON MARTIN: Take this chain as a token
                 Of the full reward which

You so justly deserve as
The bearer of this news.

> *Don Martin goes to put letters in his pocket – they fall*
> *to the ground.*

AGUILAR: I'm happy with the chain, Sir.

DON MARTIN: We'll go straight to Don Pedro.
Osorio, today is my
Wedding day and when you've
Exchanged the order I'll spend
All the gold on diamonds
For my beautiful bride.

AGUILAR: That's a modest gift for
Such a lovely wife, sir.
(Aside to Don Martin.) We're winning!

DON MARTIN: *(Aside to Aguilar.)* I'm so in love.
Oh my dear Dona Ines.

SCENE TWELVE

Dona Juana (dressed as a man) and Caramanchel.

CARA-
MANCHEL: Don Gil, I resign my post.
It's impossible to
Serve you when you are
So rarely visible.

DONA JUANA: You need sharp eyes to work
For me, Caramanchel.

CARA-
MANCHEL: I've hired a town crier
Who is hoarse from shouting:

"Whoever finds Don Gil,
Now assumed lost, last seen
Wearing a pair of green
Breeches, let him speak out.
He will be rewarded."

That's a terrifying

Cry to sponsor when all
Your pockets are empty.

I've spent two reales
On a Mass in honour
Of St Anthony; he's
Supposed to look after
All the souls who are lost.

I suspect you're a ghost
Or mixed up with a witch;
You've put the fear of God
And the Inquisition
Into me and I want my
Pay and permission to leave.

DONA JUANA: Since you last saw me I've
Been in heaven, hiding in
A house of love owned by
The most beautiful woman
In Madrid.

CARA-
MANCHEL: A woman?

DONA JUANA: Yes!

CARA-
MANCHEL: You're joking!

DONA JUANA: No!

CARA-
MANCHEL: I hope
You've got the teeth to chew
All the meat you've bitten off.

I bet it's Dona Ines,
That creature in the Duke's
Garden who was so inspired by
Your green breeches. Tell me
I'm right!

DONA JUANA: It's someone else
Who far outshines Ines though
She's her next door neighbour.

CARA-
MANCHEL: She's good?

DONA JUANA: The best!

CARA-
MANCHEL: And gives?

DONA JUANA: Everything!

CARA-
MANCHEL: And she takes?

DONA JUANA: What she's given!

CARA-
MANCHEL: Well Sir,
             Button up your purse; it's
             A magnet for women.
             What's she called?

DONA JUANA: Elvira.

CARA-
MANCHEL: No surname either? Well,
             Elvira's a nice name.

DONA JUANA: Will you take this letter
             To her, Caramanchel?

                    *Caramanchel spots letters on ground dropped by Don
                    Martin.*

CARA-
MANCHEL: There's a bundle of letters
             Here which is addressed to you.

DONA JUANA: Are you sure?

CARA-
MANCHEL: The paper's torn
             But I can just make out
             "Don Gil de Albornoz".

DONA JUANA: Show me!
             (Aside) Good Lord!

CARA-
MANCHEL: You're trembling,
             Sir, and your face is ashen.

DONA JUANA: Two seals intact, but one
             Is broken.

CARA-
MANCHEL: Who are they for?

DONA JUANA: *(Aside)* This omen tells me that
                   My victory is secure.

                   (Reads) Don Pedro de Mendoza.
                   He's the father of Ines.

CARA-
MANCHEL: This must be another
                   Proposal for the hand
                   Of Dona Ines, from
                   Someone who wants you to
                   Refer him to her father.

DONA JUANA: He couldn't have chosen
                   A better marriage broker.

CARA-
MANCHEL: Read the other address.

DONA JUANA: Agustin Solier
                   De Carmargo, city
                   Banker.

CARA-
MANCHEL: I know him, Sir,
                   He's the biggest money man in
                   The whole of Madrid.

DONA JUANA: This open letter could mean
                   Very good news for me.

CARA-
MANCHEL: Then see what it has to say!

DONA JUANA: *(Aside)* I'm sure these papers came
                   From Don Andreas and
                   Were meant for Don Martin.

                   Dona Juana reads the letter to herself.

CARA-
MANCHEL: *(Aside)* How many dishonest
                   People are there in this town?
                   A parcel pilferer?
                   Then again, there's nothing
                   More interesting than

Other people's secrets,
Especially when they only
Cost the price of postage.

Someone could have got my
Master's mail by mistake,
Had a peek at one letter
And decided to drop the lot.

DONA JUANA: *(Aside)* Fortune, you have still not
Forgotten me! How can
I lose when these letters
Have fallen into my hands!

CARA-
MANCHEL: So who are they from, Sir?

DONA JUANA: My Uncle Fernando
In Segovia.

CARA-
MANCHEL: And does
He want to marry Ines?

DONA JUANA: What a guess, Caramanchel,
How astute you are; this
Order is for a thousand
Gold escudos; he wants me
To buy her some jewels.

CARA-
MANCHEL: Oh, my ever faithful
Intuition; and will
Agustin Solier be
The redeemer?

DONA JUANA: That's what it
Says here.

CARA-
MANCHEL: Don Gil, let's go!
By the way, Sir, I'd like to
Withdraw my resignation.

DONA JUANA: *(Aside)* Oh what a lovely day.
I must find Quintana
And get him to exchange the

                    Order: now he'll discover
                    Where my schemes are leading.

CARA-
MANCHEL: I wouldn't want to lose
                    You again, Sir, so how
                    About me wearing some
                    Of those nice green breeches?

DONA JUANA: Today they will know
                    The real Don Gil.

SCENE THIRTEEN

A room in Don Pedro's house.

Don Pedro and Dona Ines.

DONA INES: I'm afraid to say, Sir,
                     You've been tricked! For the Don Gil
                     You have arranged for me
                     Is not Don Gil at all!

DON PEDRO: Ines, I am confused by
                     All these conflicting stories.
                     Did I not receive from
                     My dear friend, Don Andreas,
                     A letter confirming
                     The merit of this man?
                     And did you not just tell
                     Me you despise Don Gil?

DONA INES: His real name is Don Miguel,
                     And he's already married
                     To Dona Elvira and
                     They were both born in Burgos,
                     And she's followed him to
                     Madrid, and she's told me
                     All his lies, and she is
                     Living right next door and
                     She looks like my Don Gil.

                     You can speak to her yourself

And she'll tell you all the crimes
Of this awful Don Miguel.

DON PEDRO: Ines, I think you are
The one who has been tricked.
This signature is not false.

DONA INES: Now Sir, listen carefully:
Even though the man who
Presented that letter
To you seems convincing,
Please believe me when I
Tell you that the true Don Gil,
Whose love has touched my soul,
Is the man I saw in
The garden dressed in green,
Who because of the boldness
Of his attire, I called
Don Gil of the green breeches.

Now this man, who had heard
Very good reports of me,
Well at least of my dowry,
Was invited by your friend,
Don Andreas, to come here
And marry me and was given
As a surety that
Letter which has so fooled you!

And because as he was
Leaving he couldn't help
Speaking so passionately
Of my beauty, and my money,
His friend, Don Miguel, was quite
Consumed with envy and
A certain self interest
Which destroys all friendships,
And ignoring the fact that
He was already married
To Elvira, he forgot
All the bonds of friendship,
Why, he was actually
Staying in Don Gil's house
At the time, and stole his
Friend's letter and dressed himself

In disguise and set off
At full speed for Madrid.

And when he arrived here
Claiming to be his friend,
He presented that stolen
Letter to you and is now
Trying to force me into
A bigamous marriage!

Now the true Don Gil got
Here a few days later
And I met him in the Duke's
Garden and fell in love
With him, and he hasn't
Dared to reveal the awful
Lies of his friend because
Of course what he's doing
Is totally illegal
And he doesn't want to
Get him into trouble,
And that's why Elvira
Came to me in person
To tell me about all
The wicked lies and schemes
Of the false Don Gil whose
Advances repel me,
And she has utterly
Convinced me that all this
Is true; so you see, Sir,
What would happen if you
Married me to this monster!

DON PEDRO: Goodness me, what an awful
Lot of lies and cheating.

DONA INES: Father, it's important you
Remember all the details!

DON PEDRO: Didn't you say Don Gil was
Coming here to see us?

DONA INES: Yes, he is; Elvira
Promised he would come to
Visit me and speak to you
This very afternoon.

DON PEDRO: Well, he is late.

DONA INES: Not yet.
              (A knock.)
              I'm sure that will be him!

              (Aside) Now the hopes of my heart
              Are beginning to take wing.

SCENE FOURTEEN

Dona Juana (dressed as a man), Dona Ines, Don Pedro.

DONA JUANA: Madam, I am here to
              Humbly beg your pardon;
              I am late, and also
              In another sense I have
              Been slow to show my heart.

              During the last few days
              I've been wrestling with
              A dreadful predicament
              In which I was placed by
              A cheating liar, a former
              Friend who's stolen my name
              In a false attempt to
              Acquire my Lady's hand.

              It is not unwillingness
              Which has caused my delay;
              I must confess I fell
              In love with you the moment
              I saw you in the Garden.

DONA INES: Well I know it's all slightly
              More complicated than that,
              But now that you are here,
              Don Gil, let me introduce
              You to my father and though
              Everything's awfully
              Difficult, please help him
              To understand the plans
              Of this cruel deceiver.

DONA JUANA: Sir, I consider myself
                          Most fortunate in gaining
                          The pleasure of meeting you.
                          I would have come with less
                          Confidence had I not just
                          Received some mail from our
                          Mutual acquaintance,
                          Don Andreas de Guzman.

                          These letters will finally
                          Root out the horrendous lies
                          Of the man who robbed me
                          Of our friend's signatures
                          And tried to cheat us both!

                          Examine these documents
                          Closely, Sir, I think you'll
                          Find they confirm my claims.
                          And I urge you to guard
                          Against this Don Miguel and
                          Treat his stories with caution.

DONA INES: *(Aside to Dona Juana.)* How is he taking it?

DONA JUANA: *(Aside to Dona Ines.)* It is up to you to
                          Tell me that; you should know
                          Him better than I do.

DONA INES: *(Aside to Dona Juana.)* You seem keen to frequent our
                          Neighbourhood since yesterday.

DONA JUANA: *(Aside to Dona Ines.)* Since yesterday? Since the first
                          Time I saw you my heart
                          Has been sighing for you.

DONA INES: *(Aside to Dona Juana.)* Sighing for me?

DONA JUANA: *(Aside to Dona Ines.)* Why yes!

DONA INES: *(Aside to Dona Juana.)* And not for Elvira?

DON PEDRO: Once again Don Andreas
                          Recommends you as a most
                          Worthy husband, Don Gil,
                          I'm so glad you have come
                          At last to clear up this
                          Confusion; and if

                    You are willing today
                    Will be your wedding day.

DONA JUANA : I don't deserve to have
                    You as my father, Sir.
                    Allow me to kiss your feet.

DON PEDRO : *(Embraces Dona Juana.)* Let me take you in my arms
                    Instead, Don Gil, and greet
                    You as my son.

DONA INES :   Thank heaven!

DONA JUANA : *(Embraces Dona Ines.)* And with this embrace I'll ease
                    Any envy you may feel
                    For your next door neighbour.

DONA INES : Now I'm surrounded by
                    Your love I won't harbour
                    That ugly jealousy.

SCENE FIFTEEN

Enter Quintana.

QUINTANA : I'm looking for my master,
                    Don Gil, is he still here?

DONA JUANA : *(Aside)* Quintana, have you got
                    The gold?

QUINTANA :   *(Aside)* It's in the bag.

DONA JUANA : I'm afraid some urgent
                    Business has just arisen
                    And I must leave you for
                    A while, dearest Ines.

DON PEDRO : I trust there is no reason
                    To delay the wedding?

DONA JUANA : None at all; I'll return
                    Later on this evening.

DON PEDRO : Then Ines will be yours.

DONA JUANA : Sir, you have restored my soul!

DONA INES: What a beautiful thought!

DONA JUANA: I'll hurry back to you.

QUINTANA: *(Aside)* Every word a lie.

DONA INES: Goodbye;
            I must get to the palace.

QUINTANA: *(Aside)* Exit Juana, Elvira, Gil.

DONA JUANA: *(Aside)* Gil, Elvira, Juana, please!

SCENE SIXTEEN

Don Pedro and Dona Ines.

DON PEDRO: What a confident and
            Intelligent young man;
            I've grown to love him very
            Much already, dear Ines.

            And if that conniving cheat
            Shows his face in my house
            Again he'll suffer the
            Consequences of his lies.

SCENE SEVENTEEN

Enter Don Martin and Osorio.

DON MARTIN: Where on earth are those letters?
            Tell me, Osorio, did you
            See me drop them?

OSORIO: No, Sir.
            I can't think where they've got to.
            I remember you reading
            Them outside our lodging.

DON MARTIN: And are you sure you've searched
            Everywhere between there
            And here?

OSORIO: Everywhere in
              Every hole in the road.

DON MARTIN: Was anyone ever so
              Unlucky? All the letters
              And the money are lost.

OSORIO: Just say you've been gambling
              Instead of buying presents.

DON MARTIN: Did you look thoroughly?

OSORIO: With both eyes!

DON MARTIN: Well just go
              And look again. Maybe
              They'll turn up this time.

OSORIO: Fine chance!

DON MARTIN: No! Go straight to
              The banker and tell him to
              Put a stop on the order.

OSORIO: Now that makes much more sense.

DON MARTIN: How did a man of my
              Astuteness succeed in
              Losing vital letters?

OSORIO: Look, here comes your intended.

DON MARTIN: Today I'll ensure my
              Revenge on Ines for
              The astounding rudeness
              Of her former rejection.

OSORIO: I hope nobody else
              Has redeemed that order!

              Exit Osorio.

SCENE EIGHTEEN

Dona Ines, Don Martin, Don Pedro.

DON MARTIN: Don Pedro! Dona Ines!
              (Aside) I must try to hide my rage.

DON PEDRO: Don Miguel, is it proper
For a gentleman to
Conduct himself like the
Lowest form of criminal?
Is it proper to pretend
To be your dearest friend,
Don Gil de Albornoz
When you are none other but
Don Miguel de Cisneros?
I know full well that you
Have stolen private letters
To appropriate both his
Reputation and his bride.
Do you intend to persist
With these vile purposes?

DON MARTIN: What?

DON PEDRO: Please don't feign amazement.
You are fully aware that
Your conduct is illegal
And I shall be forced to
Take action against you
If you dare continue
To tell these brazen lies.
You are Don Miguel de
Cisneros and don't pretend
To be anyone else.

DON MARTIN: I don't know what you're talking
About, Sir.

DON PEDRO: Are you a compulsive
Liar?

DON MARTIN: I'm Don Miguel?

DON PEDRO: Yes!
And you were born in Burgos!

DON MARTIN: But it isn't true, Sir!

DONA INES: What a complete picture
Of innocence; if you don't
Honour your promise to
Dona Elvira, we shall

Inform the Officers
Of Justice of all your crimes!

DON MARTIN: Madam, Sir, I am not in
The greatest form having
Just lost a small fortune;
Who is the vicious author
Of this utter nonsense?

DON PEDRO: Your game is up, Don Miguel;
The real Don Gil has just
Left after revealing
The entire story which
Has destroyed any respect
I had for you forever.

DON MARTIN: Whoever is this Don Gil?

DON PEDRO: Don Gil the man in green.

DONA INES: Don Gil the man I love.

DON PEDRO: Don Gil the man who will
Marry my daughter tonight.
And you, Don Miguel, had
Better get back to Burgos.
Please don't feign surprise again.

DON MARTIN: Don Gil! Don Gil! May God
In heaven protect us
From the devil and Don Gil.

I swear to you some traitor
Has deceived you with this
Story; please let me speak!

DONA INES: Do not manhandle me,
Don Miguel, or we may
Be compelled to have you
Punished for your endless lies.

SCENE NINETEEN

Don Martin.

DON MARTIN: Was anyone ever so

Troubled? I am haunted
Relentlessly by Don Gil,
A man I've never seen
Yet everywhere I go
He's been and when I
Arrive he's left the scene.

My mood is now so depressed
I would give all I possessed
To catch up with this Don Gil.

I'm Don Miguel? I've never
Even been to Burgos.

SCENE TWENTY

Don Martin and Osorio.

OSORIO: We're right up the creek, Sir.

DON MARTIN: Did you speak to the banker?

OSORIO: For all the good it's done us,
             I wish I hadn't; Don Gil's
             Second name is Lucifer.
             He got there first and made
             Off with all your credit.

DON MARTIN: Don Gil?

OSORIO: De Albornoz; I
             Saw his scribbled signature.

DON MARTIN: He's trying to destroy me.

OSORIO: Solier says he's dressed
             From head to toe in green
             To make a keen impression
             On you so you won't ever
             Forget what he's stolen.

DON MARTIN: Don Gil of the green breeches
             Is determined to rob
             Me of my sanity.

             Don Gil is not a man

But an evil demon
Who's assumed human form
And my identity.

He has managed to get
Away with my mail, my wife,
And now all my money.

OSORIO: We had better go home
            Carefully, Sir, these devils
            Must know a thousand tricks.

DON MARTIN: Mary and the Saints save us
            From the devil Don Gil!

END OF ACT TWO

ACT THREE

SCENE ONE

Don Martin's lodging.

DON MARTIN: Quintana, you've said enough!
It's unbearable to know
That Dona Juana's dead.
Heaven has punished me for
My terrible cruelty,
Avarice and neglect.
She was too young to die
And it was I who killed her;
It's all my fault, Quintana,
I am her murderer.

QUINTANA: Let me tell you the story
Of her sudden tragic death.

DON MARTIN: Joy travels on leaden feet;
Sorrow arrives on winged heels.

QUINTANA: I journeyed to San Quirce
In great delight with your
Letter in my pocket,
Expecting my due reward
Which of course I didn't get.
The good sisters led me
To the grille where at last came
Dona Juana, heavy
And weary with pregnancy.

How glad I was to be
Able to cheer her with the
News of your impending visit,
That she need no longer
Question your fidelity.
The whole convent rejoiced!
My mistress read your letter
Over and over again
At least three times but just as
She had her hand in her purse

> To express her gratitude
> The abbess gravely emerged.
>
> She said she had received
> A disturbing message
> From Dona Juana's father
> Which would turn her new found
> Peace into calamity.
> He had promised to come
> To San Quirce with a sword
> To avenge his honour.
> My Lady was thrown into
> Confusion; conflicting
> Passions raged within her heart:
> Despair fought with elation,
> Fear with anticipation;
> Because of her condition
> She could not bear the strain
> And brought forth prematurely
> From the womb a little
> Girl, still not fully formed,
> Who uttered a pathetic
> First cry just as her mother
> Was struggling with her last:
> "Farewell Don Mar" she whispered
> And before she could find breath
> For the "tin" collapsed and
> Died like a tiny bird.

DON MARTIN: Please don't say any more.

QUINTANA :   My aching heart is so
             Constricting my throat
             That another word about
             This pitiful event
             Might cause it to leap out.

DON MARTIN: Now that it is all too late
            Will you, Terror, tear that
            Blind indifference from
            My soul and take its place?
            Sorrow, will you make me weep?
            Grief, must I endure you?

QUINTANA: *(Aside)* I haven't a clue where
               All these lies will end up!

DON MARTIN: It must be Dona Juana's
               Sad departed spirit who,
               Discerning my love for
               Ines, seeks to avenge
               The wicked way I've treated
               Her by taking the form
               Of Don Gil in which to smash
               All my endeavours to death.

               There's nowhere I can go
               Without the shadow of
               Don Gil; there's nothing
               I can do that he doesn't
               Try to shatter; there is
               Only one explanation:
               He's supernatural.
               What causes me to suspect
               This strange phenomenon?
               There is the fact that I've
               Searched for him in every street
               Yet never seen him once;
               There is the fact that he's
               Taken over my name;
               All this suggests to me
               That I'm haunted by the
               Angry and vengeful soul
               Of the woman I scorned.

QUINTANA: *(Aside)* Excellent! He thinks
               He's being persecuted
               By the tormented soul
               Of Dona Juana! It's
               Hilarious! And he'll
               Enjoy the joke still less
               If I play along with his
               Ridiculous delusion.

               Until this moment I've
               Dismissed all the stories
               Which have been flourishing
               Since Dona Juana died,
               Considering them fantasies

           Arising from sudden loss;
           But now you've told me how
           You sense the presence of my
           Mistress, it's difficult
           To diminish what's taking
           Place in Valladolid.

DON MARTIN: What is taking place in
           Valladolid?

QUINTANA: I'm afraid
           You will be horrified
           By these occurences:
           No one in my master's
           House has slept alone since
           The death of that ill fated
           Woman whose grieving ghost
           Is said to haunt the rooms
           Dressed in a man's clothing,
           Claiming she must traverse
           The earth as one Don Gil,
           A name she says that you
           Are using here in Madrid
           To perpetrate some scheme
           Which constantly causes her
           Enormous pain and sorrow.
           One night her father swore
           He saw her dressed from head
           To toe in emerald green,
           When she vowed to hunt you down
           Until she'd seen the end
           Of your new wedding plans.
           Although the old man ran
           Straight to the parish priest
           And made a hundred Holy Mass
           Offerings for the repose
           Of her soul, she hasn't
           Stopped appearing to him.

DON MARTIN: It is I who caused the pain
           Which wracks her troubled ghost.

QUINTANA: Is it true that you are known
           In Madrid as Don Gil?

DON MARTIN: My selfishness and greed
Have made me call myself
Don Gil, in order to
Conceal my attachment
To poor Dona Juana, for
I came here to disavow
Her, coveting instead
The worldly riches of
A match with Dona Ines.

I know I deserve to be
Punished for my betrayal,
Quintana, but part of
The blame must go to my
Ruthless and cunning father.

QUINTANA: Now I have no doubt at all
That the disturbed soul of
Dona Juana is the source
Of the frightful trouble
At home as well as the
Dangerous snares which
Beset you in this city.
Don Miguel, do you still want
To marry Dona Ines?

DON MARTIN: What choice do I have when
Dona Juana's dead and my
Mean spirited father
Insists I claim this dowry?

QUINTANA: What chance do you have when
Your matrimonial wishes
Are being censured by
A soul from purgatory?

DON MARTIN: I shall contact the convents
Of Victoria and
Carmen and implore them
To pray unceasingly for
The soul of Dona Juana;
They will surely bring peace
To her restless spirit.

QUINTANA: *(Aside)* There's so many prayers and
Masses being devised that you,

Don Gil of the green breeches,
Will soon be beatified.

SCENE TWO

In the house of Don Pedro.

Dona Ines and Caramanchel.

DONA INES: Where can I find your master?

CARA-
MANCHEL: If only I knew! I've been
Searching for him everywhere
And my eyes are sharper
Than a tailor's needle,
But no matter where I look
For young Don Gil, whose green
Breeches have me in stitches,
He's nowhere to be seen.

Tell a lie, I did catch sight
Of him not long ago but
Like money on a Friday night
He slipped right through my fingers.
He's got a little love nest
In one of these houses.

DONA INES: You mean to say Don Gil's in
Love with one of my neighbours?

CARA-
MANCHEL: Ever since I've worked for him
He's been more than keen on
Dona Elvira; he's really
Got it bad.

DONA INES: Are you sure?

CARA-
MANCHEL: Well I know he spent last night
Tucked up in her bed.

DONA INES: Last night?

CARA-
MANCHEL: Does that prick your conscience?
             Don't worry, you're one of
             Many, for despite his look
             Of innocence his morals
             Are a bit like his trousers,
             A kind of mouldy green.

DONA INES: You nasty vulgar gossip!
             That lady's reputation
             Is spotless; she is of
             Impeccable virtue.

CARA-
MANCHEL: Whether that's true or not I
             Know what I know and I know
             It from him and from this letter.
             (He shows the letter to Ines.)
             He asked me to give it to
             Elvira in person
             But she's just about as
             Elusive as Don Gil.
             I'm waiting for a servant
             To materialise to tell
             Her I'm here (there can't be
             A page in that house who
             Doesn't know what's going on).
             I came to check whether
             My master was with you.

DONA INES: This note is from Don Gil?

CARA-
MANCHEL: He wrote it all himself.

DONA INES: Well so what? It doesn't
             Have to be a love letter.

CARA-
MANCHEL: Have a peep at this lot!
             (He half opens the sealed letter and points out the bits he
             is reading.)
             I suffer from the sin
             Of curiosity
             You see, and as usual
             It got the better of me.

Does it not say here "Ines" . . .
"When I go to see" . . . "disgust" . . .
And look here "See you again" . . .
And at the side "I am yours" . . .
And at the bottom "my love" . . .
Look at the evidence!
You can judge the whole tone
From these little snippets.

DONA INES: Give it here, I'll read it all.
            (She snatches the letter from him.)
            I may as well see the truth
            Of this ungrateful cheat!

CARA-
MANCHEL: Oh don't do that! I'll be
            Right up the creek with Don Gil!

DONA INES: Be quiet, you slanderous sneak
            Or I'll get my servants to
            Give you a good beating!

CARA-
MANCHEL: Even an angry donkey
            Will only kick you twice.

DONA INES: *(Opens the letter and reads.)*
            I know no pleasure unless
            I'm sharing it with you
            And when I go to see
            Ines I am filled with
            Such sickening disgust
            I can scarcely wait until
            I see you again to tell
            You how much I love you.
            Though I must visit Ines
            This afternoon you have
            No reason to be jealous;
            I am yours forever,
            My precious one, and may
            Heaven protect you always.

DONA INES: What a nice little letter!
            And how like its chivalrous
            Author to prefer the

> Half eaten leftovers
> Of Don Miguel to Ines!
>
> So he feels disgust, my God,
> Am I so rich a dish that
> He's sick of me before he's
> Even sampled anything?
> Has Edible Elvira
> Whet his appetite for more?

CARA-
MANCHEL: Sometimes it's surprising
What a man finds tasty.

DONA INES: I am so seething with
Fury I'd like to rip
Off his ear with my teeth.

SCENE THREE

Dona Ines, Caramanchel, Aguilar.

AGUILAR: My Lady, your cousin,
Dona Clara, has called.

DONA INES: She's another victim
Of Don Gil's debauchery.

(Aside) I'll instruct Don Juan to
Kill this horrid greenfly
And I'll marry him instead.

And you can take this letter
To the woman who enjoys
The torrid pleasure he so
Delicately mentioned.
(She throws the letter to Caramanchel.)
She's hardly pure Lucrece,
But a morsel nibbled by
Someone else should satisfy
A man of his morals.

CARA-
MANCHEL: What a hot peppered temper!

Even an Englishman
Would perspire in front of her!

I don't suppose I was
The soul of discretion
In showing her this letter
But she could at least thank
Me for the information.

> *Caramanchel exits through one door.*

> *Dona Juana (dressed as a man) and Quintana enter
> through another.*

SCENE FOUR

QUINTANA: He's petitioned two convents
            To keep you in their prayers
            Because he's convinced you
            Are a soul in torment.

DONA JUANA: Well isn't that the truth?

QUINTANA: But he still intends to
            Marry Ines.

DONA JUANA: That's bad news!
            However I have just sent
            A letter to my father
            Telling him that although
            I am the legal and devoted
            Wife of Don Martin, he has
            Tragically abandoned
            Me in Alcorcon because
            Of his fatal attraction
            For one Dona Ines.

            It's quite a dramatic
            Little piece since I tail
            Off near the end saying
            I lie dying at this
            Very moment from mortal
            Stab wounds at the hand of
            My runaway husband.

Then I scratch a few words
About him taking the name
Of Don Gil de Albornoz
To avoid punishment
For my awful murder
Which had to follow my
Refusal to renounce him.

Of course I manage to
Scribble a little touch
About death being my
Just desert for my wilful
Ways and apologise for
Causing him so much trouble

And my final request,
In which I humbly appeal
To the memory of my name,
Is for his house to be
Avenged and the stain of
My dishonour washed away.

QUINTANA: But why spin such a tale
To your own father?

DONA JUANA: To get
Him to leave home and come to
Madrid to bring Don Martin
To justice for my murder.

I will use every trick
I know to vex him out
Of his lovesick fever.

QUINTANA: I hope you never have
Anything against me.

DONA JUANA: This is how we women
Seek to avenge our sex.

SCENE FIVE

Dona Juana and Dona Clara.

DONA CLARA: Don Gil, you're such a gallant

And courteous man who
Understands so well the
Needs of a lady, couldn't
You spare a day for me?
Just one day, an hour or
Even a second shared
With you is all I ask.

Like Dona Ines, I've
Got a lovely big house,
Like Dona Ines, I've
Got quite a large estate,
And like Dona Ines,
I'm very taken with you.

DONA JUANA: With me?

DONA CLARA: Yes, why not?

DONA JUANA: Dearest Dona Clara,
What a joyous blessing!
If only I'd known before!
I thought you were betrothed
To someone else and didn't
Dare approach your loveliness.

Secretly I'm rather shy
And bashful like a man
From the Basque country and
I know how very little
I matter to most people,
Which is why I never dreamed
That a woman like you
Would condescend to me!

Yet from the first moment
I saw you in the garden,
My heart belonged to you,
My salamander, for you
Stole a part of my soul
On that fateful afternoon.

But I don't know your address
Or how many more suitors
I must contend with or what
Advances you'll permit?

DONA CLARA: Don't you? Well my house is in
                    La Rue de San Luis and
                    I've got lots of admirers
                    But I've given my love
                    To a man who is as
                    Bright and green as my hope
                    And it's so hard to tell
                    You how I really feel;
                    You see he's called Don Gil.

DONA JUANA: Lady, let me kiss your hand.
                    (Dona Juana kisses Dona Clara's hand.)
                    I'm touched by your confession.
                    (Aside) I was never in such demand.

SCENE SIX

Enter Dona Ines.

DONA INES: *(To herself.)* I do wish my father
                    Wouldn't summon me when
                    I want to talk to Clara.

                    Goodness me, is that Don Gil,
                    The deceitful rat who
                    Rubs salt in my wound with
                    His exact resemblance
                    To my deadly rival?

                    He's kissing Clara's hand!
                    How bitterly sweet! Don Gil
                    Of the boyish beardless chin
                    Playing the libertine!

                    He's so spiteful! I'll stand
                    Here and listen awhile
                    To their conversation.

DONA CLARA: You say you're desperately
                    In love with me? So soon?
                    I don't believe that story.

DONA JUANA: Please don't treat me coldly;
                    I've been inconsolable

                Since the day I first saw
                You in the Duke's garden.
                You are my sun, the source
                Of my life; in the absence
                Of your light my days become
                A long and painful night.

DONA CLARA: Then why do you show such
                Interest in Dona Ines?
                You seem quite happy with her.

DONA JUANA: Happy with Dona Ines?

DONA CLARA: Yes!

DONA JUANA: I swear she is foul, false
                And frigid in my eyes; if
                She'd been christened Francisca
                She'd be blessed with all the "F's".

DONA INES: *(Aside)* How well he flatters me!

DONA JUANA: *(Aside)* What would Ines say to this?

DONA INES: *(Aside)* Clara is stupid enough
                To fall for his nonsense.

DONA CLARA: If you don't care for Ines,
                Why are you always here?

DONA JUANA: Don't you understand all
                I sacrifice for you?
                You only see the outward
                Appearance of my life
                When inside I am burning
                For you, Dona Clara.

                I didn't know where you lived
                So I endured coming to
                This ghastly house every day
                Hoping to bump into you.

DONA CLARA: I hope you're not making
                This up to hide your love
                For Ines.

DONA JUANA: Making this up?

DONA CLARA: If you really wanted my

> Address you could easily
> Have got it from Ines.

DONA JUANA: She wouldn't give it to me
Because of her jealousy.

DONA CLARA: Oh I don't care what's true
Or false any more, Don Gil,
I simply love you anyway
And can't bear you being
Cross for it makes me toss
And turn all night and cry
On my divan all day.
Please comfort me and give
Me your hand.

DONA JUANA: I give you
My hand in marriage and kiss
Yours in confirmation
Of our future union.

DONA INES: *(Aside)* Why do I suffer this man?

DONA CLARA: I must go and see my
Cousin now; Goodbye!
Come to my house later.

DONA JUANA: You make me so happy.

DONA CLARA: We'll discuss all the details
Of our wedding arrangements.

DONA JUANA: I'm not sure where I'll be
Heading next with Clara;
I'd better find Ines.

SCENE SEVEN

Dona Juana and Dona Ines.

DONA INES: Don Gil, you dissembling
Scoundrel, you three timing cheat!
I suspect Elvira is wise
To such gross behaviour

But why abuse Clara and
Myself with all these lies?

How many more wives do you
Want for your concubine,
You Turkish infidel?
Get back to Elvira,
The scraps of Don Miguel.

And be careful when you
Write letters which reveal
Your masquerade for you'll
Be left with the fruit which
Someone else has tasted.

DONA JUANA: What are you saying, my dear?

DONA INES: Your dear! Save your endearments
For Dona Elvira in
Whose bed you slept last night.
May a streak of lightning
Scar her repulsive face.

DONA JUANA: *(Aside)* Caramanchel must have
Shown her the letter which
I addressed to myself.
It's about time she bore
Some of the anguish which
I constantly endure.

What reason could you have
To slander Elvira?

DONA INES: Keep your platitudes for
Dona Clara who is well
Pleased with your proposal.

DONA JUANA: So that's why you're upset;
You must have been listening.
Didn't you realise it
Was just a silly jest?
Clara's such a foolish girl.

Darling, don't turn away;
Shine those twin suns upon me
And illuminate my soul.

DONA CLARA: Where's the joke in "I swear

                    She is foul, false and frigid
                    In my eyes"?

DONA JUANA: How can you
                    Take that seriously?
                    I was making fun of Clara.

DONA INES: What's funny about "If she'd
                    Been christened Francisca
                    She'd be blessed with all the "F's"?
                    Since you enjoy the taste
                    Of leftovers so much and
                    All I'm is "F's" to you,
                    Perhaps I should marry
                    Don Miguel after all;
                    At least he spoke well of me
                    And I'd have the pleasure of
                    Giving Elvira a dose
                    Of her own medicine;
                    A nobleman would be
                    Wasted on that woman.
                    I'll ask my father to make
                    Him my husband straight away.

DONA JUANA: *(Aside)* That doesn't sound too clever.

                    Will you punish my game with
                    Such fatal severity?
                    Ines, please listen to me.

DONA INES: I've heard enough to make
                    Me shout for a lackey
                    To throw you down the stairs
                    And straight out the front door.

DONA JUANA: I never knew you were
                    Capable of such cruelty;
                    But be assured of my
                    Fidelity and please
                    Accept my explanation.

DONA INES: Will someone come and remove
                    This abomination? Ah!
                    Don Miguel!

DONA JUANA: Has he arrived?

DONA INES: Yes! And you look terrified!

              (Loudly) Don Gil is in this house,
              The man who cheats on ladies
              Three at a time; Don Miguel,
              Come and avenge my honour
              And I will be your wife!

DONA JUANA: Listen to me!

DONA INES: Don Miguel,
              Come up here and kill Don Gil!

DONA JUANA: To hell with Don Miguel!
              I am Dona Elvira!

DONA INES: Who!

DONA JUANA: Elvira; can't you tell
              From my voice and appearance?

DONA INES: Not Don Gil de Albornoz?

DONA JUANA: Not Don Gil of anything.

DONA INES: Not another one of your
              Obscene fabrications;
              You're not Dona Elvira,
              You liar, you're Don Gil.

DONA JUANA: Our close resemblance and his
              Green clothes have deceived you,
              Dona Ines, if you're still
              Not convinced I can give
              You undeniable proof.

DONA INES: But why all the added
              Complications of dressing
              Like Don Gil de Albornoz?

DONA JUANA: I'm sad that I'm not Don Gil
              For your sake, Ines, for
              It seems we're in the same boat.

DONA INES: Can this be true? But I've
              Never seen such a likeness!

DONA JUANA: I created this disguise
              To test your affection
              For Don Miguel; I must own

A deep insecurity
Which has always provoked
Mistrust of you, Ines.

Suspecting your love for
My husband, I myself
Wrote the letter which I
Sent my servant to show you.

Of course Caramanchel
Really believed the letter
Was written by Don Gil;
I wanted him to observe
The extent of your envy
And report back to me.

DONA INES : But what did you really want?

DONA JUANA : To be sure that you loved
Don Gil and weren't planning
To take my Don Miguel.

DONA INES : It's rather confusing.

DONA JUANA : It's rather ingenious.

DONA INES : Did you really write that note?

DONA JUANA : Yes, and Don Gil lent me
This suit of green clothing;
He was keen to help me
Test your jealousy as he's
Very much in love with you

DONA INES : Very much?

DONA JUANA :   Yes, and he's
Very concerned about my
Situation with Miguel.
He wouldn't touch the food
From the plate of someone else.

DONA INES : I'm lost again.

DONA JUANA :   It's subtle.

DONA INES : So subtle and strange I still
Can't believe you're a woman.

DONA JUANA : How can I convince you?

DONA INES: I know, go and put on
A dress and I'll be able
To examine the lines
And the contours and how
It flatters your figure
And whether it fits you well
And hangs on you properly;
Why don't you try on one
Of my outfits? For I can't
Help thinking you're a man
In this suit instead of
My neighbour, Elvira.
We'll go upstairs to my room;
Clara will have gone by now.

DONA JUANA: I'm sure she went home happy!

DONA INES: *(Aside)* She says she's a woman
But she's so like a man.
My heart still refuses
To accept her story;
It tells me she is Don Gil
In speech and manner, and
In spirit and appearance.

SCENE EIGHT

Don Juan and Caramanchel.

DON JUAN: Are you the servant of
Don Gil de Albornoz?

CARA-
MANCHEL: You tell me! I serve someone
Whom I've seen rarely since
The day I was employed.
I first took up with him
Two weeks ago and in
That time I have managed
To bump into him on
A couple of occasions;
And what a master to write
Home about when I do!

As far as I know he
Owns nothing except me
And one suit of clothes which
Is entirely green; if it
Wasn't for his breeches
He wouldn't have a surname.

I can't complain about the
Money: Don Gil of the green
Breeches pays me well enough.
It's not as though I'm skint;
I've already had a lump
Sum for the little I've
Done for him: a hundred
Reales straight from the mint.

But I prefer the kind of
Master who keeps me busy:
"Caramanchel, polish
My boots; take these flowers
To Grimalda and ask her
If she slept well; find out
From Valdes what's on at
The theatre tonight", and all
Those other jobs which make
A lackey's life worth living.

I enjoy skivvying!
I don't need a master
Who never gives me orders,
Never seems to eat or sleep
And just keeps disappearing!

DON JUAN: Then he must be in love!

CARA-
MANCHEL: Well he's in it a lot.

DON JUAN: Does he love the Lady
Of the house, Dona Ines?

CARA-
MANCHEL: She loves him, but why should
That trouble him when he's
Got ready access to
An angel who lives next door?

> I haven't seen her myself
> But according to his
> Chronicles she must be
> Almost as good looking
> As I am, and that's not bad.

DON JUAN: You're extremely attractive.

CARA-
MANCHEL: It runs in the family.
> I've come here to deliver
> This note to Elvira
> But she's just like my master,
> Impossible to find and
> No one will answer the door.
> I don't suppose anyone
> Will show up now it's after
> Eleven to relieve me.

DON JUAN: So Ines loves Don Gil?

CARA-
MANCHEL: Madly enough to snatch
> This out of my hands and read
> Every word he's written to
> Elvira; she was furious!

DON JUAN: And I am madly jealous,
> Enough to lay down my life
> And everything I own
> To rid the earth of these
> Contemptible Don Gilles.

CARA-
MANCHEL: If you find them, Achilles!

DON JUAN: Death to all Don Gilles!

SCENE NINE

Dona Juana (as a woman), Dona Ines, Caramanchel.

DONA INES: Now I feel such a fool!
> I hope you can forgive

My silly little outburst.
Whatever came over me?

If only you were Don Gil!
Then I'd be delighted
With your perfect disguise
And feast my eyes upon
His lovely reflection.

Dona Elvira, you are
The exact replica
Of the man I adore!

DONA JUANA : He told me he would come
This very night to stand
Beneath your balcony.

DONA INES : Oh I do hope you're right.

CARA-
MANCHEL : *(Aside)* Someone just said Elvira!
I bet that's her with Ines;
How am I supposed to get
Out of this predicament?
It must have been set up
By the devil himself.

I've got to pass a love
Letter from my master
To Elvira right under
The nose of Ines who
Knows precisely what it says.
Careful Caramanchel,
I can smell a couple
Of beautiful black eyes.

DONA INES : Hello, what do you want
In this house?

CARA-
MANCHEL :   Madam, are you
Dona Elvira?

DONA JUANA :   Yes.

CARA-
MANCHEL : Jesus, Mary and Joseph!
Don Gil in women's clothes!

                    Sir, you can look for someone
                    Else to carry your bags
                    From now on; Gil by day,
                    By night a Gillian!
                    Well fuck me! Oops, sorry!

DONA JUANA : Are you quite sane? What are
                    You saying?

CARA-
MANCHEL :   I'm saying that
                    You, Sir, are a man dressed
                    As a woman as sure
                    As the Lord God made this world
                    In six days and rested
                    On the seventh, Amen.

                    I'm saying that you're Don Gil!

DONA JUANA : You think that I'm Don Gil?

CARA-
MANCHEL :   I do, as God's my witness.

DONA INES : I'm not the only one who's
                    Been fooled by this resemblance.

CARA-
MANCHEL :   Here in Spain you can be
                    Whipped for doing less than
                    What you're doing; I never
                    Saw a man who was more of
                    An insult to womenkind.

DONA INES : I think you'll find this lady
                    Is Dona Elvira.

CARA-
MANCHEL :   Would you like me to call you
                    Sir or Madam, Master or
                    Mistress? It doesn't matter,
                    I'm handing in my notice.

                    I'm not hanging around
                    A boss in pretty frocks,
                    You might start wanting me
                    To wear one of your dresses;
                    Caramanchel's a lackey

And not a lackeyess.
Me with a transvestite
For a master? No thanks!
Where I come from eating
Meat and fish together
Is not considered right.

So I'd like to terminate
Our arrangement now, Sir.

DONA JUANA : You are understandably
Alarmed by my resemblance
To your master, though it
Is the very reason why
He loves me so dearly.

We were also astonished
When we first met by the
Extraordinary mystery
Of our similarity;
Yet our minds and interests
Are so alike that we soon
Formed a unique friendship:
We trust each other deeply.

Ines, you understand so
Well the nature of my
Relationship with Don Gil;
Please try and explain it
To this nice gentleman.

DONA INES : Well lots of people do say
That close resemblance is
A cause of love.

CARA-
MANCHEL :   Not that close.
Madam, do you take me for
A complete idiot?

DONA JUANA : Don Gil will arrive here
In one hour to give you
The opportunity of
Seeing us both together
And then what will you say?

CARA-
MANCHEL: I'll say anything you like!

DONA JUANA: When he comes you can speak
            To him and humbly beg
            My pardon.

CARA-
MANCHEL: In an hour?

DONA JUANA: You will be quite startled.

CARA-
MANCHEL: I'm not saying anything.

DONA JUANA: Wait for him in the street
            Outside the doorway of
            This house; Ines, let's go
            On to the balcony
            And look out for Don Gil.

CARA-
MANCHEL: I'll be right below you!
            *(He secretly slips the letter to Dona Juana. Aside to Dona
            Juana.)* Here's a letter from
            My master; I couldn't
            Deliver it before
            In front of Dona Ines.

DONA JUANA: Oh that's all sorted out now.

CARA-
MANCHEL: *(Aside)* Whether that's Don Gil or
            Dona Elvira, something's
            Going on around here.

SCENE TEN

A street.

Don Juan (dressed for night).

DON JUAN: I came here to kill one
            Or other of the men
            Who are frustrating my

Matrimonial hopes
And are known as Don Gil.

As there are two, at least
One of them will appear
Here soon to serenade
His lady and I intend
To cure him of his love-
Sickness tonight and make
Sure he never sings again.

It's either me or them!

SCENE ELEVEN

Don Juan and Caramanchel.

CARA-
MANCHEL :   I came here to meet the
Elusive Don Gil, that's if
He puts in an appearance.

Even if he does show up
And stand next to Elvira,
Such evidence might not be
Entirely conclusive.

SCENE TWELVE

Dona Juana (as a woman) and Dona Ines appear at a window.

DONA INES :   It's extremely warm tonight.

DONA JUANA : Warm weather breeds warm hearts.

DONA INES :   Are you certain Don Gil
Is coming to see us?

DONA JUANA : Do you still doubt his love?

(Aside) Valdivieso should call
For me any minute now.
Then I can change my clothes
And return as Don Gil.

DON JUAN: *(Aside)* I'll listen to their love talk
              However painful for me.
              That's the voice of dear Ines;
              She must be by the window.

DONA INES: I can hear someone below;
              Perhaps it's our Don Gil?

DONA JUANA: Speak to him and find out.

CARA-
MANCHEL: *(Aside)* There's someone else about;
              I wonder if it's Don Gil.

DON JUAN: *(Aside)* Come here and confess your name.

DONA INES: Is that Don Gil down there?

DON JUAN: *(Aside)* If that's the name she wants
              To hear, I will answer yes.

              (Muffled) Yes, I am Don Gil who
              Comes to declare his passion.
              My Lady, when I first
              Set eyes on you I froze
              In the white heat of my love.

DONA INES: Are you insinuating
              In rather inordinate
              Language that you find me cold?

CARA-
MANCHEL: *(Aside)* This is a deep voiced Don Gil.
              My master's pitch is higher,
              Unless it broke yesterday.

DON JUAN: Let me gaze upon you,
              Fair daughter of the sun.

DONA INES: How can I be hot and cold?

DON JUAN: Love inflames passion while
              Doubts fill the heart with ice.

DONA JUANA: *(Aside)* I'm sure this is Don Martin.
              You wretched man! How you
              Waste the precious time that
              We might spend together.

DONA INES: *(Aside)* That can't be my Don Gil.

You down there, are you the
Don Gil of the green breeches?

DON JUAN: Don't you recognize me?

CARA-
MANCHEL: *(Aside)* I certainly don't, young man.

DONA INES: As there's two of you, I can
Sometimes get a bit confused.

DON JUAN: Naturally, but tell me,
Which one do you prefer?

DONA INES: You of course, although the things
You've said tonight have made me
A little uncertain.

DON JUAN: I'm disguising my voice and
Hiding my face because this
Is a rather public place.

SCENE THIRTEEN

Don Martin (dressed in green) and Osorio.

DON MARTIN:*(Aside to Osorio.)* I don't care if the man
Ines says she prefers
Is the anguished soul of
Dona Juana (which is
Quintana's explanation
For the disasters which
Befall me) or if I'm
Tormented by another
Suitor who's stolen my name
To test her loyalty.

The point, Osorio, is that
I'm mad with jealousy;
Can Ines have fallen
In love with someone else
With more worthy prospects?

OSORIO: That's not possible, Sir.

DON MARTIN:You know how distinguished

I am in Valladolid;
I'm from the finest family,
The noble blood of Guzman
Courses through my veins
And I'm extremely wealthy.
I know it's indelicate
To even mention money
But it does have some bearing
On this situation.

I have no explanation
For the charms of this Don Gil,
Whoever he might be,
Other than his green breeches.
She professed from the first
A liking for this colour
And if that's what pleases her
I'll go out and get a pair.

Osorio, from now on
I'll be seen to wear only
The favoured shade of green.

OSORIO: If I may be so, Sir,
            That's a ridiculous
            Suggestion.

DON MARTIN: What do you say?

OSORIO: You're not very well, Sir.

DON MARTIN: Well or not well I'll don
            His dress and be known as
            Don Gil of the green breeches.

            You may as well go home;
            I want to have a word
            With Dona Ines' father.

OSORIO: Then I'll see you later.

SCENE FOURTEEN

Dona Juana, Dona Ines, Don Martin, Don Juan, Caramanchel.

DONA INES : *(To Don Juan.)* Don Gil, your attentions
           Are so fitful while my love
           For you is so faithful.

DON MARTIN: *(Aside)* Don Gil! At last I shall
           Come face to face with the man
           Who thwarts my intentions.
           But what shall I do if
           It is Dona Juana?
           The fear I might contest with
           A tormented soul turns my
           Courage into cowardice.
           I've always vowed never
           To mix with the occult:
           That would be to doubt the
           Existence of the devil.

DONA INES : It looks as if someone else
           Is down there now.

DON JUAN :   I'll go
           And find out who it is.

DONA INES : But why?

DON JUAN :   Because, dear Ines,
           He's standing within earshot
           Of us and I should advise
           Him to move somewhere else.
           Don't worry, I won't be long.
           Good Evening!

DON MARTIN: Who's that?

DON JUAN :   Move on!

DON MARTIN: Where would you have me go
           When my home is in this house?

DON JUAN : *(Aside)* I know that voice; this is
           Don Gil de Albornoz,
           Whom Ines despises.

CARA-
MANCHEL : *(Aside)* A policeman would be
           Useful at this juncture.

DON JUAN : Don Gil, let us discover

            If you are green or yellow!
            The moment has arrived
            Which I have long desired
            And you have long denied.

DON MARTIN: *(Aside)* How did he recognise me?
            My God, no human eye
            Could have seen through this disguise!
            So my fearful fantasies
            Are made real by the ghostly
            Presence of Dona Juana.

DON JUAN: Don Gil, it's time to prove
            The fire of your love with
            The cold steel of a sword!
            For to court a damsel
            And to flee from a rival
            Is the seal of a coward!

CARA-
MANCHEL: *(Aside)* Another Gil? Who knows?
            These Gilles must come in pairs.
            This one's not my Gil though;
            Mine crows like a little cock.

DON JUAN: Don Gil, draw out your sword!

CARA-
MANCHEL: *(Aside)* There's two or I'm insane.

DONA INES: There's a new Gil about.

DONA JUANA: That's my Miguel no doubt.

DONA INES: You're absolutely right.

DONA JUANA: *(Aside)* How many men use my name?
            I don't know this one at all.

DON JUAN: Sir, unsheath that blade or
            I'll be forced to break the rules.

DON MARTIN: I will never use my sword
            Against the sacred dead
            Nor waste my strength in combat
            With an immortal spirit;
            I fight with souls and bodies
            That are still united.

DON JUAN: Are you suggesting that
                I'm so shaken by you that
                My soul has left my body?

DON MARTIN: If you are near the throne
                Of God, which in all faith
                I believe, what do you want
                Of me, Dona Juana?

                If you are still on your
                Journey to salvation,
                I'll have more Masses said
                To help you on your way.

                I confess before you
                My selfishness and blame;
                If only my love could bring
                You back to life I could bear
                The weight of all these sins.

DON JUAN: What are you saying, Sir?
                That I am Dona Juana?
                Dead? That I'm a dead woman?
                I'm a soul in torment?

DONA JUANA: *(Aside)* What a gorgeous moment!

CARA-
MANCHEL: *(Aside)* The living dead! Santa
                Susana, Santa Elena!

DONA INES: Elvira, what's happening?

DONA JUANA: There's a lunatic out there!
                Let's be quiet and listen.

CARA-
MANCHEL: *(Aside)* Anguished spirits at midnight;
                Jesus, I'm really scared!

DON JUAN: Don Gil, I demand once
                Again that you draw your sword
                Or I'll be driven to some
                Dishonourable action.

CARA-
MANCHEL: I wish someone would turn me
                Into smoke so I could
                Escape up a chimney stack.

DON MARTIN: Oh Innocent Soul, I beg
                    You in the name of the
                    Passionate love which bound
                    You to me on earth and which
                    Floods into my mind with such
                    Bitter sweet remembrance,
                    Please forgive me, let your
                    Righteous anger and my
                    Punishment cease at once.

                    I know that you have taken
                    Human form and called yourself
                    Don Gil to obstruct my
                    Marriage and cause me shame.

                    I know that you also
                    Haunt Valladolid dressed
                    In a green suit with the
                    Promise to avenge your name.

                    But I implore you in the
                    Memory of our nameless
                    And ill fated little girl
                    Whose miscarriage brought about
                    Your death and filled your house
                    With blackest mourning, please
                    Let me rest now; don't give me
                    Any more sleepless nights!

                    Oh Soul in torment, how can
                    Jealousy exist in death?
                    Is it revenge which binds
                    You to purgatory?
                    I swear on my life,
                    Whether you're in heaven
                    Or in hell, whatever
                    Trickery you invent,
                    Ines will be my wife.

                    Exit Don Martin.

SCENE FIFTEEN

Dona Juana, Dona Ines, Don Juan, Caramanchel.

DON JUAN :   So he has gone, having
              Evaded my challenge
              With the most bizarre excuse
              Anyone has ever heard.

CARA-
MANCHEL :   (*Aside*) Caramanchel, you've been
              A lackey to a soul
              In torment; what a break:
              So that's why I could never
              Find the man, for Christ's sake!

DONA JUANA : Dear friend, I must leave you
              For a moment to deal with
              A little household problem;
              Valdivieso beckons me;
              You carry on with your
              Delightful chat with Don Gil.

DONA INES :   It's so dark! Let me fetch
              A maid to see you home.

DONA JUANA : I only live next door;
              There's no need.

DONA INES :   Please take a cloak.

DONA JUANA : No Ines, I'll go without
              A cloak and without a soul.

                    Dona Juana withdraws from the window.

DON JUAN :   Now to find the young Don Gil;
              I'm sure he'll turn up tonight.

DONA INES :   Don Gil, your courage exposed
              You to incredible risk.

DON JUAN :   Love is not true without
              Courage but a mere charade.
              Listen, more people approach.

SCENE SIXTEEN

Dona Clara (dressed in green breeches), Don Juan, Dona Ines, Caramanchel.

DONA CLARA: *(Aside)* Jealous pain has driven fear
Out of my heart, and I've dressed
As a man to test the truth
Of Don Gil's protestations,
And I think I look quite smart!
I want to see if he comes
Here tonight to see Ines,
And if he does I'll know
That I have been betrayed.

DON JUAN: Wait there, I'll see who it is.

DONA CLARA: *(Aside)* There's someone at the window;
I need to get closer to
See if it's Ines waiting
For Don Gil, and if it is
I'll pretend to her that
I am he; it's the only
Way to calm the tempest
Which rages in my heart.

Fair Lady up above me,
Does Don Gil have permission
To offer you words of love?
Since I have given you
My heart, surely I may
Express my hopes which are like
My breeches, bright and green.

CARA-
MANCHEL: *(Aside)* Another Gil has rained down
From heaven; that makes three!
This street's awash with Gilles.

DONA INES: *(Aside)* This is my dearest Gil;
I love his sweet little voice;
Clearly until now I've
Been swapping pleasantries
With the shameless Don Juan.

DON JUAN: *(Aside)* This is the Gil who turns
Her head!

DONA INES: *(Aside)* I'm so worried!
Don Juan is dreadfully

Impulsive; he might murder
The man I really love.

Don Juan approaches Dona Clara.

DON JUAN: Don Gil, how convenient
              To meet you in this quarter;
              Come and get what you deserve.

DONA CLARA: What a nerve! Who dares to
              Address me in this way?

DON JUAN: Your executioner!

DONA CLARA: My executioner?

DON JUAN: Correct! And though you've tried
              To make Ines believe
              That I am Don Miguel
              I will break your spell on
              Her and make her my wife.

DONA CLARA: I must have been tempted
              By the devil to come here.
              Oh poor Clara; you'll end up
              Stabbed to death by a knife.

SCENE SEVENTEEN

Dona Juana (dressed as a man), Quintana, et al.

DONA JUANA: *(To Quintana.)* I've come to talk to Ines
              At her window; I don't know
              What on earth will happen next.

QUINTANA: For one thing your father
              Has just arrived in town.

DONA JUANA: This means he's convinced that
              I lie dead in Alcorcon;
              He should be around shortly
              To accuse Don Martin
              Of my brutal murder.

QUINTANA: Without a doubt, my Lady.

DONA JUANA: We're not alone, Quintana.

QUINTANA: Stay here, I'll find out who's there.

DONA CLARA: You say you are Don Gil?

DON JUAN: Yes, and I court fair Ines.

DONA CLARA: How very interesting.

DONA JUANA: Dear Sirs, may I come past?

DON JUAN: Who asks?

DONA JUANA: Don Gil!

CARA-
MANCHEL: *(Aside)* That's four!
            There's no end to them; there
            Could be thousands more!

DON JUAN: We have
            Two Gilles here already.

DONA JUANA: So with me there will be three.

DONA INES: Another Gil? Good Lord!
            At least one of you must be
            The man I love so dearly.

DON JUAN: It's me, I am Don Gil,
            The man with green breeches.

DONA CLARA: *(Aside)* My fear has changed to rage!
            How could he come to her
            Window and forget all
            His words of love to me?
            Clearly they were shallow.
            He'll get my revenge now!

            Don't you know me, Ines?
            I am Don Gil, the one
            With the brightest green breeches.

QUINTANA: *(Aside to Dona Juana.)* You've started a new fashion;
            There are two men in green here
            Fighting over your name.

DONA JUANA: Excuse me but I'm Don Gil
            In your favoured suit of green.

DONA INES: Oh heaven, how exciting!

DON JUAN: I'll defend this window
                With my life; go away
                Or I'll run you through!

DONA JUANA: Those are fighting words, Sir.

QUINTANA: Let's put them to the test.

CARA-
MANCHEL: Death to all Green Gilles!

                Fight – Quintana wounds Don Juan.

DON JUAN: Oh my God, I am dead.

DONA JUANA: Let that be punishment
                For your grossly arrogant
                Presumption; and you can
                Tell Dona Ines that
                You were wounded by the
                True Don Gil: Proficient
                Swordsman and Prince in Green.

                Exit Dona Juana, Quintana, Don Gil.

DONA CLARA: *(Aside)* I'm leaving with my heart
                Twisted into jealous knots;
                He gave his hand to me;
                He's got to keep his promise!

                Exit Dona Clara.

DONA INES: Don Gil has wounded a man
                For me! It's ecstasy!

                Exit Dona Ines.

CARA-
MANCHEL: To hell with all four Gilles;
                I've seen enough of them.

                So the lovesick soul who
                Hired me has come back from
                The other world to cure
                Her jealousy with this
                Curious form of revenge.

                The cold dawn is about to
                Break along with my mind.
                Jesus, Jesus, I'm going

Mad in the head; I've been
Lackey to the living dead!

SCENE EIGHTEEN

San Jeronimo Street.

Don Martin (dressed in green).

DON MARTIN: Oh Streets of this great city,
Mimics of Babel's madness,
Worn away with endless lies,
Cosseting the rich whilst
Castrating the poor; oh you
Brothels, constantly filled
With pain and corruption,
Tell me who in heaven could
Want to cause me so much harm?
Will a Gil always haunt me?

You Trees who clothe these streets
With fallen leaves and whose
Branches sway with lovers'
Trophies, if I was to hang
A token upon you t'would
Be an emblem of grief.

You Joyous Fountains whose
Gentle droplets bless the earth
Beneath you, whose waters
Whisper secrets, will I al-
Ways be pursued by a Gil?

Tell me the crimes I have
Committed which cause even
My shadow to hate me?
Does my adoration
Of Ines deserve the
Invisible torments which
Continuously taunt me?

Who is this Don Gil who
Frustrates all my desires?
Why is he named after me?

Why does he constantly
Follow me? Does he mean
To tell me there'll always
Be a Gil behind me?

If I court Dona Ines,
Gil courts Dona Ines,
And so he wins her love;
If my father sends me
Letters, Gil apprehends
The letters and uses them
For his wicked schemes;
If I receive money,
Gil steals all the money.
I don't know where to go
Because there'll always be
A Gil there before me.

SCENE NINETEEN

Don Diego, Quintana, a Policeman, Don Martin.

QUINTANA: *(To Don Diego.)* That man is the false Don Gil;
              (To one side.) Back at home he is known as
              Don Martin de Guzman,
              It was he who murdered
              Your daughter, Dona Juana.

DON DIEGO: I would like to stain my white
              Hair red with his evil blood;
              One who carries such shame
              Is not of noble birth.
              Officer, arrest this man!

POLICEMAN: My Lord, surrender your sword.

DON MARTIN: Me?

POLICEMAN: Yes, you.

DON MARTIN: Who to?

POLICEMAN: The law.

Don Martin hands over his sword.

DON MARTIN: What new vexation is this?
Why do you arrest me, Sir?

DON DIEGO: You traitor, how can you
Feign shock, having cruelly
Murdered your ill fated wife?

DON MARTIN: I don't possess a wife!
Has someone been murdered?
Once I gave my word to a
Woman in Valladolid
But then I left and came here.

I was informed that she
Was pregnant and retired
To a convent where she died
Giving birth prematurely
To a little girl, but
That doesn't make me her
Murderer; Quintana,
Speak, you are my witness.

QUINTANA: Don Martin, I can only
Witness to the fact that
You stabbed your wife to death
In Alcorcon without cause.
Heaven cries out for your crime
To be brought to justice.

DON MARTIN: I swear by God you are
A traitor.

POLICEMAN: What's all this?

DON MARTIN: If I had my sword I would
Cut out your lying tongue
And your treacherous heart.

DON DIEGO: Criminal! Murderer!
Don't deny what is clearly
Written in this letter.

Don Martin reads the letter to himself.

DON MARTIN: This is Dona Juana's hand.

DON DIEGO: Read her last words carefully.

DON MARTIN: Jesus, I don't understand.

                    It says I stabbed my wife
                    In Alcorcon; I've never
                    Even been to Alcorcon.

DON DIEGO: Don't start wasting our time
                    With pathetic excuses.

POLICEMAN: You can prove your innocence
                    From a prison cell, Sir.
                    You should have plenty of
                    Time to construct a case.

DON MARTIN: This letter complete with
                    Signature spells out that
                    She was confined within
                    The cloisters of San Quirce;
                    So tell me how I could have
                    Murdered her in Alcorcon?

DON DIEGO: Because the letter you've
                    Produced is a forgery
                    Exactly like your name.

SCENE TWENTY

Don Antonio and everyone already on stage.

DON
ANTONIO: *(Aside)* This is Don Gil; I'd
                    Know him anywhere by
                    The colour of his breeches.

                    (To Don Martin.) I am here to ensure that
                    You honour your promise
                    Of marriage to my cousin,
                    Dona Clara, as I'm
                    Given to understand,
                    Don Gil, that your actions
                    Have since betrayed your words.

DON DIEGO: Without question it was
                    The love of this woman which
                    Caused him to kill his wife.

DON MARTIN:Please give me back my sword

And I will end my life
Since my torments know no end.

DON
ANTONIO: Dona Clara loves you;
She needs you; you're her
Husband; you must live for her.

DON MARTIN: And who is Dona Clara?

DON
ANTONIO: What an evasion! Are you
Don Gil or not?

DON MARTIN: That's what
I'm called in Madrid, but not
Don Gil of the green breeches.

DON
ANTONIO: But those are green breeches.
Don Gil, either you must
Marry my cousin or feel
The full force of the law.

DON DIEGO: The executioner will
Stick his deceitful head
Upon a spike in the square.

DON
ANTONIO: What harm has he done you, Sir?

DON DIEGO: He has murdered his wife.

DON
ANTONIO: Traitor!

DON MARTIN: Oh Death, they threaten
Me with your power yet
I beseech you to come
And bring peace to my soul.

SCENE TWENTY ONE

Fabio, those already on stage.

FABIO: *(To Policeman.)* Take this dangerous man away
                And throw him into jail.

DON MARTIN: Is there still more to suffer?

POLICEMAN: He's on his way already,
                Sir, of what crime do you
                Accuse him?

FABIO: In the early
                Hours of this morning outside
                The respectable house of
                Don Pedro de Mendoza,
                This man attacked and wounded
                Don Juan de Teledo.

DON MARTIN: I have attacked Don Juan?

QUINTANA: Just look at how he squirms.

DON JUAN: Who is Don Juan? What wound
                Did I inflict? Which house?
                When? What attack is this?
                Why am I endlessly
                Being persecuted?

                Listen to me; what I am
                Going to tell you may
                Shock you but it is the truth:
                I am being haunted and
                You are all being tricked
                By the unquiet soul of
                Dona Juana who has passed
                Unwillingly into
                The other world only
                To return to this one
                Daily for her revenge
                On me because of the crimes
                I committed against
                Her when she was alive.

DON DIEGO: So you confess you killed her.

POLICEMAN: Come along to prison now!

QUINTANA: Just a moment, I see some
                Ladies alighting from
                A carriage and heading

Fast in our direction.
They're bound to supply us
With vital information.

SCENE TWENTY TWO

*Dona Juana (dressed as a man), Dona Ines, Dona Clara (as a woman),
Don Juan (with a bandaged arm).*

DONA JUANA: Father, how good to see you here!

DON DIEGO: Who are you?

DONA JUANA: Your daughter,
          Juana!

DON DIEGO: Alive?

DONA JUANA: Alive!

DON DIEGO: Is this not your letter?

DONA JUANA: I wrote it to get you
          To hurry to Madrid
          Where Don Martin had been
          Masquerading as Don Gil
          So that he could marry
          This lady, Dona Ines,
          To whom I've now explained
          The whole story and she's
          Very happy to furnish
          Us with the solution
          To our strange malady.

          I played the false Don Gil,
          Famous for green breeches
          And a soul in anguish.

          Don Martin, I've heard
          You dwell in fear and dread
          Of my soul; if that's still
          The truth, give me your hand.

DON MARTIN: I kiss yours in relief
          And astonishment for
          In seeing you anew

                    I see the end of my
                    Persecutions: even
                    Quintana was against me.

DONA JUANA: He protected my honour.

DON MARTIN: Can you forgive me, Sir?

DON DIEGO: Let me embrace you as
                    A father; the time I
                    Was your enemy and wished
                    To see you dead has passed.

DON PEDRO: At last I understand all
                    The confusing intrigues
                    Of the various Don Gilles,
                    Not to mention Juana
                    And the charming Elvira.

                    The injury suffered by
                    Don Juan is but a flesh wound.

DON JUAN: It's healed by Dona Ines
                    Who's agreed to marry me.

DONA INES: You're my Lord and Master.

DONA CLARA: I know I was fooled by
                    Don Gil of the green breeches
                    But so was everyone else!

DON DIEGO: Don Martin, you are my son.

DON MARTIN: Then I must summon my
                    Father to celebrate my
                    Marriage to Dona Juana.

SCENE TWENTY THREE

*Caramanchel, with little candles covering his hat and breeches, dressed in
pictures of saints, with a pot around his neck and an aspergillon.*

CARA-
MANCHEL: Everyone must pray to
                    Bring peace to the wounded
                    Soul of my master who's

> Forced to walk this earth in
> A pair of green breeches.
>
> I entreat you by all
> The encrusted sores of
> Every plague infested
> Sanatorium in Spain
> To keep away from me,
> Go back! Go back!

DONA JUANA: Are you
> Quite well, Caramanchel?
>
> I am your Don Gil: my soul
> Is in my body and my
> Body is in my soul.
> Take a look at these people;
> They're not afraid of me.

CARA-
MANCHEL: Are you a man or a woman?

DONA JUANA: A woman.

CARA-
MANCHEL: Well that's enough
> To confuse the universe.

SCENE TWENTY FOUR

Osorio.

OSORIO: Don Martin, your father
> Has arrived in Madrid.
> He's waiting for you
> At his lodging house.

DON MARTIN: Let us all go to welcome
> Him and celebrate
> This double wedding.

DONA JUANA: And end the story of Don Gil,

CARA-
MANCHEL: A comedy of green breeches.

THE END